D1517578

Catch of the Day

200+ Easy Recipes for the Everyday Angler

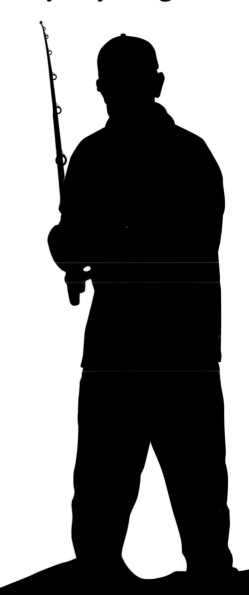

Chef John Schumacher

Creator of The Game Gourmet Seasonings

©2009 John Schumacher

Published by

kp **krause publications**
A subsidiary of F+W Media, Inc.

700 East State Street • Iola, WI 54990-0001
715-445-2214 • 888-457-2873
www.krausebooks.com

Our toll-free number to place an order or obtain
a free catalog is (800) 258-0929.

All rights reserved. No portion of this publication may be reproduced
or transmitted in any form or by any means, electronic or mechanical,
including photocopy, recording, or any information storage and retrieval
system, without permission in writing from the publisher, except by a
reviewer who may quote brief passages in a critical article or review to
be printed in a magazine or newspaper, or electronically transmitted on
radio, television, or the Internet.

Library of Congress Control Number: 2008909286

ISBN-13: 978-1-4402-0237-7

ISBN-10: 1-4402-0237-0

Designed by Kara Grundman

Edited by Corrina Peterson

Printed in China

DEDICATION

This book is dedicated to adventurers, and especially to my son Carlton, who is the most passionate fisherman and talented home cook I know.

Chef John Schumacher

FOREWORD

My professional and personal life is centered around food. Cooking is my gift and I love to share it with family, friends, customers and audiences. I also love the adventures and challenges of fishing and have been fortunate to have amazing experiences in a variety of locations, all of which have shaped my love of fish cookery.

"Catch of the Day" was born of a desire to demystify fish cooking, encourage creativity and to share my philosophies and insights on recipes, techniques and equipment. It is not a coffee-table book but rather a practical, cook-friendly resource with recipes that work and chef hints that allow the reader to personalize and enhance their dishes.

The recipes showcase the versatility of fish without being too complicated or intimidating. They expose new possibilities and encourage cooks to regionalize the dishes. The recipes are flexible with several types of fish that can be used with one recipe. The lists of ingredients are not overly long or exotic and can be found in most grocery stores.

This cookbook addresses the basics of cooking fresh water versus salt-water fish, textures, flavors, sizes and the little extras – side dishes, spices and sauces – that make a difference in the final product. My success is your success!

CONTENTS

DON'T OPEN THE BASKET, DAD

I am a motor boating, live bait casting, daredevil and buck tail using man. On a family vacation at a trout fishing lodge my 12-year-old son Carlton discovered his inner fly fisherman. I was not so fortunate.

Standing in a peaceful trout stream, I whipped the long fly rod towards a school of bait-shy fish. The crafty trout whizzed by like the Blue Angels. This frustrating scenario repeated itself over and over again, with Carlton advising and critiquing my technique. Cold brews did little to improve my skill or attitude.

After six long hours, Carlton had patiently and skillfully managed to catch three shiny brook trout, which he placed in a trout basket and carefully anchored in the slow-moving stream.

As he moved further upstream to get away from my chaotic fishing attempts he said, "Don't open the basket, Dad. They will jump out. This is our supper and I only have to catch one more fish." He repeated his instructions several times and made me solemnly promise that I would not open the basket.

As he moved out of sight, curiosity got the best of me. With one eye on my son and one eye on the top of the basket, I opened the lid just an inch or two to peek inside. Whoosh! Out jumped a shiny blue trout. All I could think as it swam away was, "Oh no-o-o-o-! Come back here!" Was it a mirage? I went to re-examine the basket and whoosh, another trout jumped out!

Guilt and panic set in as I scoured the shoreline desperately trying to find worms, dynamite, anything that would help me replace the missing fish. No luck.

When Carlton returned with his last fish the basket was missing. I told him that I'd already taken the trout to the lodge cook to be cleaned and prepared for our supper. I volunteered to bring his last fish to the kitchen while he put away his gear.

Usually the lodge has extra trout on hand for guests who are unable to catch their dinner. I was counting on that to bail me out but the freezer was empty. As we sat down for dinner, I still hoped for a miracle. The server placed a platter of two trout and roasted vegetables on the table to feed my wife, daughter, son and me.

Carlton shot a glance my way. I looked at the platter and said, "Maybe the kitchen lost one and one escaped out of the basket." Carlton's eyebrows raised skeptically and I knew I was in trouble.

The confession and punishment followed: No trout for Dad. I ate a lot of bread, vegetables and humble pie that evening.

Breakfast

- This dish is a winner for camp cooking. Be careful not to burn the recipe if using an open fire or camp grill.

Potluck Fish Breakfast

10 hard-cooked eggs, peeled and quartered
1 lb. fresh asparagus, cut into 1-inch pieces
½ c. butter
½ c. flour
1 c. ham, cut into ¼-inch cubes
1 c. fresh mushrooms, sliced ¼ inch thick
½ tsp. salt
⅛ tsp. white pepper
½ tsp. ground nutmeg
4 drops Tabasco sauce
3 c. milk
1 c. chicken or fish stock (see recipe p. 47)
4 large or 12 small fried fish fillets, cut into 3-inch squares
1 c. cheddar cheese, shredded
8 biscuits (see recipe p. 219)

Cook, peel and quarter eggs. Discard tough ends of asparagus. In a large skillet, combine asparagus and butter. Heat until butter comes to a fast bubble. Add flour to pick up butter. Reduce heat. Let cook for 2 minutes, stirring often to keep from sticking. Add ham, mushrooms, salt, pepper, nutmeg, Tabasco, milk and stock. Bring to a boil. Reduce heat to low. Let simmer 5 minutes, stirring to keep from sticking. Place fish fillets on top of mixture. Press down gently to submerge. Add egg pieces and top evenly with cheese. Cover tightly. Turn off heat. Let stand for 10 minutes. Serve over fresh biscuits or sourdough toast cut into ½-inch cubes.

Serves 4 to 6.

ANGLING TIP

Wash your hands. If your bait smells like bug spray, sunscreen or gasoline the fish are less likely to bite.

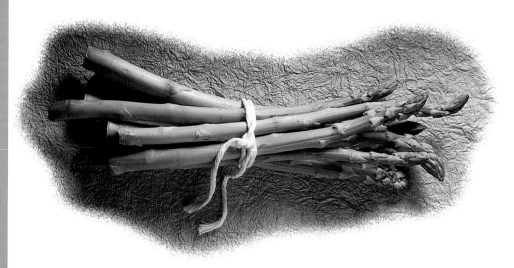

Campfire Breakfast Fish Pizza

pizza crust mix or frozen pizza crust
2 large red onions, cut into ½-inch slices
2 large boiled potatoes, sliced ¼ inch thick
8 tomato slices, ½ inch thick
6 large fresh mushrooms, sliced ½ inch thick
olive oil spray
¼ c. vegetable oil
8 panfish fillets
1 c. seasoned flour (see recipe p. 181)
¼ c. butter
8 eggs, scrambled
salt and pepper to taste
1 c. cheddar cheese, shredded
hot chili pepper (optional)

(see recipe p. 181)

Make pizza crust dough according to directions on package. Set aside for later. Take onions, cooked potatoes, tomatoes and mushrooms and spray with olive oil. Set on grill over campfire on medium heat. Turn vegetables as needed to keep from burning. When hot and golden brown, set to the side of the grill to keep warm.

Heat an iron skillet hot and add vegetable oil. Place fish fillets and flour in a plastic bag; shake gently to coat. Remove fish fillets and place in skillet. When all fillets are in pan, add butter and fry fillets until golden brown on both sides. Remove fish to a paper-towel-lined plate to keep warm.

Evenly flatten pizza crust to about 1/2 inch thick. Spray with olive oil on both sides. Place on campfire grill until golden brown on bottom. Turn and cook other side until golden brown. Brush with butter or olive oil. Set to the side of the grill to keep warm.

In another skillet, scramble eggs to medium hardness. Do not overcook. Add salt and pepper to taste. Place pizza crust on a large plate or platter. Layer potatoes, tomatoes, mushrooms and onions on top of crust. Arrange fish fillets evenly over vegetables. Top with scrambled eggs, cheddar cheese and sliced chili pepper, if desired.

Serves 4.

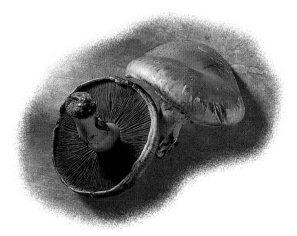

CHEF'S TIPS

• For 4 hungry fishermen you will need to use two pizza crusts. If you have time, make your own pizza crust (see recipe p. 212).

• Be careful not to burn crust or vegetables over too hot a campfire.

• For lunch, instead of scrambled eggs, add a can of cream-style corn, heated.

• I love salsa with this recipe. You may add anything you like. It's your breakfast.

ANGLING TIP

Panfish more actively feed at sunrise and sunset. However, they are sometimes cooperative during the entire day, especially if the water is cloudy.

Catfish and Shrimp
Over Grits

Catfish and Shrimp Over Grits

½ c. flour
1 T. Cajun seasoning
1 T. vegetable oil
2 catfish fillets, whole or cut into 2-inch squares, ½ inch thick
1 T. butter
¼ c. green onions, sliced into ¼-inch rounds
2 c. fresh mushrooms, sliced ¼ inch thick
1 T. fresh tarragon, chopped medium
2 c. peeled, uncooked shrimp
½ tsp. salt
¼ tsp. black pepper
1 T. balsamic vinegar
1 tsp. Worcestershire sauce
4 c. grits (see recipe p. 224)

Combine flour and Cajun seasoning in a shallow bowl. Heat oil hot in a large skillet. Dredge fish fillets in Cajun flour. Shake off excess flour. Place fish in skillet. Add butter. Brown fillets until golden. Turn. Slide fillets to one side of the pan.

Add green onions, mushrooms and tarragon. Cook until mushrooms and scallions are tender. Add 1 teaspoon Cajun-seasoned flour to make a slightly thick sauce. Stir to combine. Add shrimp, salt, pepper, balsamic vinegar and Worcestershire sauce. Bring to a boil. Remove from heat. Cover and let steep for 5 minutes. Place a large mound of grits in the center of a dinner plate. Make an indentation in the center of the grits. Top with catfish, vegetables and shrimp sauce.

Serves 4.

CHEF'S TIPS

• Catfish fillets should not be more than ½ inch thick. If they are too thick, slice them in half.

CHEF'S TIPS

- The trout fillets will cook very quickly.
- Any thin, boneless fish fillets will work in this recipe.
- I like to add a little sour cream to this dish.
- The tortilla shell is not only excellent with fish, it covers the plate and helps cut down on the dishwashing.

Skillet-Poached Eggs and Trout Fillets in Tomato Salsa

2 T. olive oil
1/2 c. onions, diced into 1/4-inch pieces
2 cloves garlic, minced fine
1 large red pepper, diced into 1/4-inch pieces
1/2 c. dry red wine
1 1/2 c. tomato salsa
1/3 c. fresh cilantro, chopped coarse
black pepper to taste
4 4- to 6-oz. trout fillets
8 large eggs
4 large, soft tortilla sheets

In a large iron skillet or Dutch oven, heat olive oil. Add onions, garlic and red pepper, and cook until onions are tender. Add red wine, salsa, cilantro and pepper. Bring to a boil. Add trout fillets and place around the edges of the pan. Place the eggs in the center of the skillet. Return to a simmer for 5 minutes. Remove from heat and cover 2 to 3 minutes, or until eggs are cooked to your liking. With a large spoon, remove fish, eggs and sauce. Place on a tortilla-shell-lined plate.

Serves 4.

Skillet-Poached Eggs
and Trout Fillets in
Tomato Salsa

CHEF'S TIPS

• You may substitute instant potatoes for mashed potatoes.

ANGLING TIP

Prevent snarled messes of tangled fishing rods in your boat by sewing long, skinny "socks" to slide over them when they're not being used.

Fishballs

2 c. mashed potatoes (see recipe p. 205)
1 lb. boneless, skinless
fish fillets
1 T. butter
1 c. red onion, diced fine
¼ tsp. black pepper
2 eggs
1 egg yolk
¼ tsp. salt
¼ tsp. lemon zest, shredded fine
1 tsp. poultry seasoning
½ c. Parmesan cheese, freshly grated
4 drops Tabasco sauce
½ c. seasoned flour (see recipe p. 181)

Cook potatoes. Drain and let steam off well. Mash. Do not add any extra ingredients as they will make the potatoes too soft. Set aside to cool.

Dice fish fillets into very small pieces. In a small skillet, heat butter to a fast bubble. Add onions and sauté until tender. Do not brown. Add fish. Combine well. Remove from heat. Cover and let sit off the stove for 10 minutes. Place in a large mixing bowl. Add remaining ingredients except mashed potatoes and seasoned flour. Combine well.

Add potatoes to make a dough. It should have the same consistency as mashed potatoes. If the consistency is too loose, add dry instant potatoes or more Parmesan cheese. Cover and place in a refrigerator to cool and firm. Form into walnut-sized balls. Roll in seasoned flour, then shake off excess flour.

Heat an electric skillet to 375°. Fry 5 to 6 fishballs at one time. Do not overbrown. Remove with a skimmer to a paper-towel-lined bowl. Season with celery salt or your favorite seasoning. Serve with scrambled eggs or as an appetizer.

Serves 4.

Country Fish with Hash Browns

¼ c. melted butter
8 slices whole wheat bread with crust removed
4 large or 10 small boneless fish fillets
4 boiled potatoes, cooled and shredded
2 10¾-oz. cans cream of celery soup
2 c. colby cheese, shredded
1 c. sour cream
¼ c. fresh chives, diced fine
¼ c. cheddar cheese, shredded
1 c. tomatoes, diced into ¼-inch pieces

Preheat oven to 350°. In a Dutch oven or baking dish, add butter. Place two layers of whole wheat bread on the bottom. Top with fish fillets, side by side, as close as you can place them without overlapping.

Combine all remaining ingredients and pour over the top of the fish fillets. Cover and cook in a 350° oven for about 1 hour. If you are cooking over an open grill, hang the Dutch oven on a hook away from the hot fire so the bottom of the pan does not burn.

Serve with eggs and additional diced tomatoes.

Serves 4.

CHEF'S TIPS

• This works well with salmon and all saltwater fish.
• If you have a stiff upper lip about the cream of celery soup, take 1 pint medium cream sauce (see recipe p. 178) and add 1 cup peeled, finely diced celery.

Heartland Fish Hash

¼ c. olive oil
½ c. red onion, diced into ¼-inch pieces
½ c. celery, sliced ¼ inch thick
1 c. red pepper, diced into ¼-inch pieces
2 c. red potatoes, boiled with skins on, diced into ¼-inch pieces and cooled

1 c. frozen whole-kernel corn
½ c. dill pickles, diced
1 tsp. dry thyme
1 tsp. salt
black pepper to taste
2 c. fish fillets, sliced 1 inch thick

In a large skillet, heat oil until hot. Add onions, celery and red peppers. Sauté until onions are tender. Add potatoes, corn, pickles, thyme, salt and pepper. Toss to combine and cook on medium heat until the potatoes and corn are hot. Place fish pieces evenly over the base and cover. Cook on low heat for 3 minutes. Remove pan from heat and let sit, covered, for 5 minutes. Remove cover and serve with poached or boiled eggs.

Serves 4.

ANGLING TIP

In addition to picking up vibrations with sensitive nerve endings, bass use smell to detect prey or predators.

Breakfast Fish
Soufflé

Breakfast Fish Soufflé

1½ c. half-and-half
½ c. onion, diced into ¼-inch pieces
½ c. celery, diced ¼-inch pieces
½ c. red pepper, diced into ¼-inch pieces
1½ tsp. fresh thyme
6 peppercorns
1 clove garlic, quartered
1 c. boneless, skinless fish, cut into ½-inch cubes
¼ c. butter
2 T. flour
1 T. German mustard
pinch salt
pinch white pepper
8 oz. sharp cheddar cheese, shredded
5 egg yolks
7 egg whites, at room temperature
1 T. Parmesan cheese

Preheat oven to 350°. Place half-and-half, onion, celery, red pepper, thyme, peppercorns and garlic in a saucepan and simmer for 3 minutes. Be careful not to boil. Remove from heat and let stand for 15 minutes to infuse flavors. Strain and keep liquid. Place strained liquid in a small saucepan. Add cubed fish. Simmer for 3 minutes. Remove fish to a bowl and let cool.

In a saucepan, heat butter to a fast bubble. Stir in flour and cook for 1 minute, stirring constantly. Remove from heat. Stir in strained liquid, whisking smooth with a wire whisk. Place mixture back on heat and cook until it is a smooth, thick sauce. Add mustard, salt, white pepper and shredded cheddar cheese. Remove from heat. Let cool for 5 minutes. With a wooden spoon, stir in egg yolks, one at a time, until well blended.

In a clean bowl, beat egg whites until stiff. Add cheese base slowly by folding into the stiff whites with a wire whisk. Gently combine, being careful not to overmix.

Butter and flour a 2½-pint soufflé dish. Add half the egg mixture. Very gently place fish cubes evenly in the mixture. Top with remaining mixture. Bake in a 350° oven for 30 minutes. Sprinkle Parmesan cheese over top and continue baking for 10 minutes. Soufflés should be served at once.

Serves 4.

CHEF'S TIPS

- To prepare soufflé dish for baking, brush its sides and bottom with soft butter. Place two tablespoons of flour in the dish and shake it so that the flour is evenly distributed on sides and bottom. Pour off excess flour.

- It is important not to overbeat egg whites. They should be stiff, but not dry.

- The reason you have more egg whites than egg yolks is to increase the volume of the soufflé.

- Gently combine cheese base with whites. Be very careful not to overmix, as mixing takes the air out of the whites.

CHEF'S TIPS

- It is important that the roe is taken from fresh fish.
- Smaller roe from panfish is excellent. It takes less cooking time.
- This recipe can be used as an appetizer. Spread sour cream on pumpernickel toast and top with fish roe.

CHEF'S TIPS

- All smoked fish work well with this recipe.
- If you are feeling like you own Park Place or Boardwalk, serve with sour cream and caviar.

Fish Roe

fresh fish roe (6 large slabs or 12 to 16 small slabs of roe)
1 qt. ice-cold water
2 tsp. salt
1 c. seasoned flour (see recipe p. 181)
8 strips bacon, diced ½ inch thick
1½ c. onions, sliced ¼ inch thick
1 tsp. fresh lemon juice
1 T. capers, drained

Remove roe from fish, keeping it all intact in its own clear sack. Place salt in ice cold water. Place roe in salted water. Let sit for 10 to 20 minutes. Remove from water and gently coat with flour.

While roe is chilling, heat a heavy frying pan over medium-high heat. Add bacon and fry until golden brown. Add onions and cook until transparent. Push bacon and onions to one side. When the fat starts to bubble, gently add floured roe. Sauté until golden brown. Gently turn roe and splash with lemon juice. Top with onions and bacon pieces. Add capers. Cover and remove from heat. Let sit for about 2 minutes. Remove cover and test for doneness. When roe is done, it will have a medium-orange color all the way through.

Serve with scrambled eggs and fried potatoes for breakfast.

Serves 4.

Fishermen's Quiche

9-inch pie crust (see recipe p. 213)
¼ c. green onions, sliced
½ c. Farmer's cheese, shredded
½ c. cheddar cheese, shredded
1½ c. fish fillets, sliced ½ inch thick
1 c. fresh mushrooms, sliced ½ inch thick
½ c. red peppers, sliced ½ inch thick
¼ c. diced dill pickles
4 eggs
2 egg yolks
1½ c. half-and-half
¼ tsp. dry thyme
1 tsp. salt
¼ tsp. pepper

Preheat oven to 375°.

Make pie crust dough. Roll out dough to ⅛-inch thickness and place in a 9- to 10-inch pie plate. Place onions, cheeses, fish, mushrooms, red peppers and dill pickles in the pie plate. In a bowl, whisk the eggs, yolks, half-and-half, thyme, salt and pepper to a smooth liquid and pour over filling. This will be a very full pie. Put in the oven on a baking sheet or cookie pan.

Bake in a 375° oven for about 45 minutes, or until set. Let stand 10 minutes. Serve with salsa.

Serves 4.

NOTES

ALASKAN BEAR SNACK

For my 40th birthday, I had the good fortune to spend the month of October on the Aleutian Islands Peninsula. The trip was planned to include fishing during the silver salmon run.

The location was remote. There were no roads and small two-seater floatplanes were the only means of transportation. Along the way we saw dozens of crashed planes. The pilot said, "There are good flying days and bad flying days." I was hoping for a good one.

The pilot flew about an hour towards a fast flowing river that fed into an inland lake. The river was about 25 yards wide. He landed the plane on the water, taxied towards the beach, and threw my rubber raft into the water so I could paddle to shore. He pointed to the location where I should fish and said he would be back in about four hours to pick me up.

He then said, "Do not stray, and watch out for the bears. If they come by, let them eat the fish you have on the line and don't keep any fish on shore." Despite my protests that I had no weapons to protect myself, he repeated his instructions and off he flew.

The fishing was spectacular. In just over an hour, I caught nine 15-pound silver salmon. Then I noticed some movement to my far left and saw a young brown bear lumbering toward me. He was fat and putting the finishing touches on his physique in preparation for winter.

I moved from the shore to a shallow point in the river and caught and released some small fish. The bear was watching me closely. It became apparent that he was lazy and had no intentions of getting wet to catch some fish.

At this point, the bear moved to within 15 feet of me. As I hooked the next salmon, I heard a low roar, let out the line and jerked it upwards into the air towards the bear. With one powerful movement, he swatted the salmon off my hook, confiscated the fish and left the same way he came. I decided that he wasn't a lazy bear; he was a smart bear and this was just an afternoon snack. He left my line and lure intact and I went back to fishing.

When I returned to camp later that evening and told the story, the outfitters shook their heads and said, "Chef, that was a little close. You'd better stay in the kitchen before you become the bear snack."

Appetizers

CHEF'S TIPS

• Northern pike, salmon or lake trout are perfect for this recipe. Saltwater fish can also be used.

ANGLING TIP

Typical smelt spawning runs last seven to ten days beginning in late April or early May.

Pickled Fish

STEP A:
Prepare Fish
8 c. raw fish fillets, cut into 1-inch cubes

STEP B:
Make Brine Solution
1 c. pickling salt
6 c. water

STEP C:
Cover with 1 qt. white wine vinegar

STEP D:
Prepare Pickling Solution
$1/2$ c. brown sugar
1 c. white wine
$3/4$ c. white vinegar
2 T. pickling spice
1 small jalapeño pepper, seeds removed
1 tsp. juniper berries, crushed
2 tsp. fresh tarragon leaves
$1/2$ c. white wine

STEP E:
Add Vegetables
$1/2$ c. diced onion
$1/4$ c. diced red pepper

Fillet and skin fish making sure to remove all large bones. (Small bones will dissolve.) Cut into cubes (Step A). Put cubes in glass dish and cover with brine solution (Step B) for about 24 hours. Remove brine and rinse well with cold water. Put cubes back into dish and cover with white vinegar (Step C). Cover dish and refrigerate for 48 hours.

Drain and rinse in cold water. Put fish cubes in large glass jar. Make pickling solution (Step D) by bringing pickling ingredients to a brisk boil for 3 minutes then cool to 160°. Add to fish. Add the onion and red pepper (Step E).

Cover and refrigerate for five days, stirring or shaking jar once a day. Keep refrigerated and serve with crackers, cheese, sliced apples or rice cakes (see recipe p. 211).

Serves 10 to 12.

• *The pickling solution must be cooled to 160°. If the pickling solution is too hot, it will parcook the fish, making it mushy. If the pickling solution is too cold, it will not kill unwanted bacteria and the pickling flavor will not permeate the fish cubes.*

Fish Deviled Eggs

1 dozen extra-large eggs
12-oz. bottle beer
2 c. boneless, skinless fish fillets, cut into small pieces
1 T. German mustard
1/2 c. mayonnaise
1/8 tsp. black pepper
1 tsp. Worcestershire sauce
4 drops Tabasco sauce
2 T. fresh chives, sliced paper-thin
1 T. horseradish, squeezed dry

Boil, peel and chill eggs. Cut in half the long way. Remove yolks and place in a bowl. Wash cooked egg whites gently. Place egg whites inside down on a cotton towel to dry.

In a medium skillet, heat beer to a simmer. Add fish pieces. Simmer for 5 minutes and remove from heat. Let steep for 5 minutes. Remove fish pieces with a skimmer and place on a paper-towel-lined plate. Place in refrigerator to cool. When fish pieces are cool, mash with a fork, removing any remaining bones.

In a medium bowl, mash egg yolks. Add mashed fish, mustard, mayonnaise, pepper, Worcestershire sauce, Tabasco sauce and chives. Combine well. Turn egg white halves upright. Place a small amount of horseradish in the bottom of each egg half. Top with a generous amount of filling.

To serve, place 1/2 teaspoon deviled fish mixture on top of a cracker. This will stabilize the egg. Set the fish deviled egg atop the cracker. Garnish with diced hot pepper or black olive slices.

Makes 24 deviled eggs.

CHEF'S TIPS

- Leftover cooked fish can be used in place of raw fish.
- When using pickled fish, be sure to pat dry.
- For a unique presentation, serve atop chilled rice cakes (see recipe p. 211)

ANGLING TIP

Perch feed primarily near the bottom. Try using worms, small minnows, insect larvae or crayfish tails on a small hook with light tackle.

**Bass and Water
Chestnut Strudel**

Bass and Water Chestnut Strudel

¼ c. sesame oil
½ c. zucchini, cut into matchstick-sized pieces
½ c. summer squash, cut into matchstick-sized pieces
½ c. carrots, cut into matchstick-sized pieces
½ c. red peppers, cut into matchstick-sized pieces
1 c. fresh wild mushrooms, cut into matchstick-sized pieces
½ c. green onions, cut into matchstick-sized pieces
1 T. fresh ginger, minced fine
2 c. bass fillets, cut into 1-inch strips
½ c. water chestnut slices, drained
1 bunch cilantro leaves
2 tsp. soy sauce
⅛ tsp. black pepper
8 phyllo dough sheets (see recipe p. 214)
½ c. clarified butter (see recipe p. 189)
½ c. egg wash (see recipe p. 181)

Heat sesame oil smoke-hot in a wok or large iron frying pan. Add all vegetables and ginger. Sauté for 2 minutes. Add fish, water chestnuts, cilantro, soy sauce and black pepper. Remove from heat. Cover and let sit for 5 minutes. Remove and place in colander to drain and cool.

Brush each sheet of phyllo dough with clarified butter, building a 5- to 8-layer crust. Spread chilled fish mixture evenly over dough, leaving a 1-inch strip on each side and 2-inch strip on the bottom. Lightly brush side and bottom strips with egg wash. Fold side strips over filling. Starting at the top, roll the dough toward the bottom as with making a jelly roll.

Line a baking pan with aluminum foil. Place strudel on pan seam side down. Lightly brush the top of the strudel with a thin coat of egg wash. Pierce strudel 4 times to let steam escape. Bake at 350° for 25 minutes. Cut into 4 diagonal pieces. Place on a warm serving plate. Serve with your favorite sauces.

Serves 4.

CHEF'S TIPS

- This is an excellent recipe for strong-flavored or oily fish.
- Olive or peanut oil can be substituted for sesame oil
- To reheat, microwave strudel on high for 20-30 seconds.

ANGLING TIP

Watch the weather: The best time to fish for bass is before a front comes through.

• Fish cubes must be
handled gently to
retain their shape. If
you are not concerned
with the shape, use
whole panfish fillets.

ANGLING TIP

Catfish don't strike like
most fish; let them take
the bait, and wait up
to ten seconds before
setting the hook.

Sautéed Fish with Almond Pesto

¼ c. clarified butter (see recipe p. 189)
4 c. boneless, skinless fish fillets, cut into 1-inch cubes
1 c. seasoned flour (see recipe p. 181)
2 tsp. fresh lemon juice
1 c. almond pesto (see recipe p. 186)

Heat clarified butter in a large skillet until hot. Gently coat fish
cubes with seasoned flour and shake off excess. Place each fish cube
in skillet and sauté on all sides until golden brown. Sprinkle evenly
with lemon juice.

Heat a large dinner plate. Cover the bottom of the plate with
warm almond pesto. Top with fish cubes.

Serves 4.

Catfish and Potato-Stuffed Pimientos

4 white baking potatoes
2 tsp. salt for boiling water
1 clove garlic
2 c. catfish, cut into 1-inch cubes
1/2 c. sour cream
1/2 tsp. salt
1/8 tsp. black pepper
1/4 c. salted sunflower seeds
1/4 c. red onions, diced fine
8 fresh pimientos

Preheat oven to 350°.

Peel potatoes and cut into quarters. Place in salted water. Add garlic clove. Boil potatoes uncovered until almost tender. Add catfish and boil 3 to 5 minutes longer. Drain off water and let potatoes and fish steam off for 5 minutes. Add sour cream, salt and pepper. Mash the fish and potato mixture, leaving some chunks for texture. Add sunflower seeds and onions. Combine.

Remove stem end, seeds and white membrane from pimientos. Gently fill pimientos with fish mixture. Lay in a lightly greased baking pan. Leave enough space between pimientos to allow them to bake evenly. Bake in a 350° oven for 20 minutes, or until filling is hot.

Serves 4.

CHEF'S TIPS

- Pimientos are a variety of sweet-flavored, large, heart-shaped red peppers.
- Four red peppers can be used if pimientos are not available. They must be used stem side up.
- For a spicier flavor, use four poblano peppers.

Fish Nachos

2 c. fresh tomatoes, diced into 1/4-inch pieces
1 c. dill pickles, diced into 1/4-inch pieces
6 c. extra-large corn chips
2 c. cooked fish fillets, cut into 1-inch pieces
1/3 c. black or green olives, sliced thin
1/2 c. guacamole
1/2 c. sour cream
1 c. sharp cheddar cheese, shredded
1/2 c. salsa
1/2 c. green onions, cut 1/4 inch thick
2 to 3 chili peppers of your choice, sliced 1/8 inch thick

Preheat oven to 375°.

Place diced tomatoes and pickles in a strainer. Drain off excess liquid. Place corn chips in an ovenproof serving dish. Top with fish, tomatoes, pickles, olives, guacamole, sour cream, cheddar cheese, salsa, green onions and chili peppers.

Bake in a 375° oven for 15 minutes. Remove and serve.

Serves 4.

CHEF'S TIPS

- Two to three cups of shredded lettuce can be added to this recipe before adding cheddar cheese.

CHEF'S TIPS

- This dish can also be used as a main course.
- I enjoy sprinkling mozzarella cheese over the shells for the last 5 minutes of baking.

ANGLING TIP

Panfish use very specific areas of a lake: Concentrate your efforts on outside weed edges, openings in weed beds, fish cribs and tree falls.

Italian Fish-Stuffed Shells

12 jumbo pasta shells
12 boneless, scaled panfish fillets
2 tsp. lemon pepper
12 mozzarella cheese sticks, 1/2 inch thick and 1 1/2 inches long
1 T. olive oil
1 c. red peppers, cut into 1/2-inch cubes
2 cloves garlic, minced fine
2 c. fresh mushrooms, cut in half
1 qt. spaghetti sauce of your choice
1/2 c. dry red wine
12 tomato slices, cut 1/2 inch thick

Cook pasta according to package, making sure not to overcook. Rinse in cold water and drain well.

Preheat oven to 350°.

Sprinkle fish fillets with lemon pepper. Wrap fillet around cheese stick and gently place inside shells. Place shells open side up in a roasting dish. In a skillet, heat olive oil. Add red peppers, garlic and mushrooms. Sauté for 2 to 3 minutes. Add spaghetti sauce and red wine. Bring to a boil. Top shells with sauce. Cover dish and bake for 15 to 20 minutes in a 350° oven.

To serve, place shells atop a 1/2-inch-thick tomato slice.

Serves 4.

Sautéed Fish Livers with Red Onion Confiture

1 lb. fresh fish livers
1 pt. milk
2 c. red onion confiture (see recipe p. 198)
$^1/_2$ c. seasoned flour (see recipe p. 181)
$^1/_4$ tsp. ground allspice
$^1/_2$ tsp. fennel seeds, ground fine
$^1/_4$ tsp. salt
$^1/_8$ tsp. white pepper
1 T. clarified butter (see recipe p. 189)
$^1/_4$ c. shallots, diced $^1/_4$ inch
$^1/_2$ c. cream sherry

Clean all silver skin, fat and veins from fish livers. Soak in milk for at least 1 hour in refrigerator. Remove livers to a strainer and shake gently to remove excess liquid.

Heat red onion confiture in a saucepan and set aside.

Combine seasoned flour, allspice, ground fennel seeds, salt and white pepper in a pie plate. Roll livers in flour mixture and coat well. Shake off excess flour. Heat a skillet with clarified butter to medium-hot. Add shallots and sauté until shallots are transparent. Add livers and sauté for 1 minute. Turn and sauté for 1 minute on other side. Add sherry and simmer for 1 minute. Serve on $^1/_2$ cup warm red onion confiture.

Serves 4.

CHEF'S TIPS

- The key to success for this recipe is to quickly sauté the fish livers to medium-rare on both sides and serve immediately.

ANGLING TIP

Trolling is by far the best method for catching Coho salmon. Good choices for trolling baits include plugs, spoons, and dodgers with flies.

Mushrooms Kathleen

Mushrooms Kathleen

12 large mushroom caps
1½ lbs. butter or margarine
¼ c. cooked bacon, crumbled
¼ c. minced shallots
1 T. chopped parsley
¼ c. garlic powder, or 6 cloves garlic, minced
12 large sea scallops

Preheat oven to 350°.

Wash and dry mushrooms, removing the stems. Place mushrooms hollow side up in a baking dish. Allow butter or margarine to soften. Add bacon, shallots, parsley and garlic, and stir to combine well. Place 1 teaspoon garlic butter mixture in mushroom cap and top with one scallop. Cover each with one rounded tablespoon garlic butter mixture. Bake in a 350° oven for about 20 minutes or until golden brown. Serve with toast points.

Serves 4 to 6.

CHEF'S TIPS

- This is the most popular appetizer at our restaurant.
- Pine nuts can be substituted for bacon.
- For more complexity, add 1 escargot per mushroom cap.
- For fish-stuffed mushrooms, use 1-inch boneless, skinless fish cubes.

Gravlax

1 6- to 8-lb. salmon
⅓ c. salt
⅓ c. brown sugar
3 T. fresh dill weed, or
1 T. dry dill weed

2 T. black pepper, coarsely ground
¼ tsp. ground allspice
2 tsp. juniper berries, mashed medium

Scale and fillet fish. Lightly run a flat hand over inside of the fillet to find pin bones. Remove pin bones with a needlenose pliers.

Lay salmon fillets skin side down on a cotton dish towel or double-thick piece of cheesecloth. Combine remaining ingredients. Spread evenly over both salmon fillets. Place 1 fillet over the other, skin side up. Roll tightly in cloth and place in a flat baking pan. Place a flat pan over the top and add 5 lbs. of weight, distributing the weight evenly over the fillets. Refrigerate for 24 hours. Remove from refrigerator. Drain off excess liquid. Turn fish over and repeat the process for 3 more days.

To serve, remove salmon fillets from cloth. Brush off curing spices. Slice thinly on the bias. Serve with capers, shallots, sour cream and rye toasts.

For storage: Cut fillets in half. Place in double-thick resealable plastic bag. Add 1 oz. vegetable oil to help keep fish soft. Freeze flat. Use fillet within 90 days.

Each fillet of salmon serves 6 to 8.

CHEF'S TIPS

- If you are not a fan of juniper berries, leave them out.
- I also enjoy gravlax on chilled rice cakes (see recipe p. 211) for an international crossover cuisine.

Fish Rockefeller Wellington

¼ c. butter
1 clove garlic, minced fine
½ c. shallots, diced into
¼-inch pieces
1 c. fresh, small mushroom caps, cut into quarters
½ c. seasoned flour
(see recipe p. 181)
10-oz. package frozen spinach, drained well
1 T. minced anchovy fillets

½ c. heavy cream
½ c. Parmesan cheese, freshly grated
⅓ c. fresh bread crumbs (see recipe p. 181)
½ tsp. salt
⅛ tsp. black pepper
12 puff pastry sheets
½ c. egg wash
(see recipe p. 181)
12 panfish fillets

Preheat oven to 375°.

Heat butter to a fast bubble. Add garlic, shallots and mushrooms, and sauté until shallots are tender. Add seasoned flour and stir with a wooden spoon to make a thick sauce. Add spinach, anchovies and heavy cream, and stir to combine. Add Parmesan cheese, bread crumbs, salt and pepper. Combine well. Place in a bowl and keep refrigerated until needed.

On a cutting board, cut puff pastry sheets into 3-inch squares. Brush each square lightly with egg wash. Place 1/2 tablespoon of spinach filling in center of each square and top with fish fillets. Top fish fillets with 1 tablespoon spinach filling and cover with a second square of puff pastry. Seal sides shut with a fork. Pierce a small hole in center to release steam. Place on a baking sheet. Brush top lightly with egg wash and bake at 375° for 15 to 20 minutes.

Serves 4.

ANGLING TIP

If you hook a big pike and then lose him, just wait a little while. Their appetites are so strong that they forget quickly and start to feed again.

Dill Poppyseed Blini with Smoked Fish

1 ¼ c. half-and-half
3 T. German mustard
2 large eggs
2 T. olive oil
1 ¼ c. all-purpose flour
1 ½ tsp. poppy seeds
1 tsp. dry dill weed
2 tsp. baking powder
½ lb. thinly sliced smoked fish
½ c. sour cream
caviar to taste

In a bowl, place half-and-half, German mustard, eggs and olive oil. Whisk well. Combine all dry ingredients. Add to liquid ingredients and stir to a smooth batter. Cover and place in the refrigerator for 30 minutes.

Set an electric frying pan or griddle to 375°. Lightly wipe the surface with oil or vegetable spray. Using a tablespoon, place batter on griddle. Blini should be silver dollar size. Cook blini like pancakes, browning on both sides.

To serve, top blinis with thin slices of fish, sour cream and caviar.

Serves 4 to 6.

Lacey Cheese Fish Roll-Ups

¼ c. clarified butter
(see recipe p. 189)
6 boneless, skinless fish fillets
½ c. seasoned flour
(see recipe p. 181)
½ c. red onions, diced into
¼-inch pieces
½ c. black olive pieces
6 artichoke hearts, cut in half
1 ½ c. salsa
2 c. Monterey Jack cheese, shredded fine
1 c. Swiss cheese, shredded fine

Heat butter in a skillet. Dredge fish fillets in seasoned flour. Shake off excess flour. Put fish fillets in skillet and fry until golden brown. Set on a paper-towel-lined baking dish. Cover fish to keep warm.

To make warm salsa mixture, place onions, black olives and artichoke heart halves in a skillet and cook until onions are tender. Add salsa and bring to a boil.

Heat an electric frying pan or griddle to 400°. Lightly brush with clarified butter. Combine Monterey Jack and Swiss cheeses and place ½ cup cheese mixture on hot griddle. Let melt to a thin circle. When cheese turns golden brown on the bottom, top with a fish fillet and ¼ cup onion/salsa mixture. Fold in half and put on a warm serving plate. Serve with remaining warm salsa mixture.

Serves 4.

CHEF'S TIPS

• Be sure to use high-quality caviar.
• Pickled fish or gravlax can be substituted for smoked fish.
• Capers can be substituted for caviar.
• Diced onions may be added when garnishing. First, place the diced onions in a towel and squeeze out the liquid. This will reduce the onion's pungent effects without removing the crunchy texture.

ANGLING TIP

Crappies hang out in the shallows during their spring spawn, and move to deeper water during the summer.

NOTES

BRANDI'S BIG FISH

My daughter's first big fish was a 1.3-pound sunfish that hung in the bar at our hotel for years. She thought I was crazy for getting that fish mounted, comparing it less than favorably to her brother's trophy walleye hanging right next to it. It just didn't make sense to her that such a small fish was mounted. She thought I did it because I felt bad for her and wanted to encourage her to continue fishing.

Years later, after working in the fishing industry, she came back to the hotel for a family visit and rediscovered that sunfish on the wall. She finally understood why I did it – It was a big beauty. She was so proud that it now it hangs in her office and she smiles every time she sees it.

Soups & Chowders

CHEF'S TIPS

• Gently remove
fillets with a slotted
spoon, because
when poached they
become very tender.

• If you have several
kinds of fish available
(such as salmon
or panfish fillets),
combine them in
this soup.

Chunky Fish Vegetable Soup

1 T. olive oil
3 stalks celery, cut into 1/2-inch cubes
1 jumbo onion, cut into 1/2-inch cubes
2 carrots, cut into 1/2-inch cubes
1 qt. chicken stock (see recipe p. 47)
2 bay leaves
1 tsp. salt
1/4 tsp. black pepper
2 potatoes, cut into 1/2-inch cubes
2 c. whole tomatoes
1 red pepper, cut into 1/2-inch cubes
1 c. zucchini, cut into 1/2-inch cubes
1 tsp. fresh thyme
1 T. chopped fresh basil
1 c. dry white wine
4 2- to 3-lb. boneless fish fillets, or 20 panfish

In a medium-sized soup pot, heat olive oil. Add celery, onion
and carrots. Sauté until onions are transparent. Add chicken stock,
bay leaves, salt, pepper, potatoes, tomatoes, red pepper, zucchini,
thyme, basil and white wine. Simmer for 30 minutes. Add fish fillets.
Simmer for 2 minutes. Remove bay leaves. Serve soup in bowls
topped with fillets.

Serves 8 to 10.

CHEF'S TIPS

• This stock is for
poaching or boiling
fish and shellfish.

• To intensify flavor,
cook down liquid until
it is reduced by half.

Court Bouillon (Vegetable Stock)

1 c. carrots, cut into 1-inch cubes
1 c. red onion, cut into 1-inch cubes
1 c. celery, cut into 1-inch cubes
3 1/2 qts. water
1 qt. dry white wine
1 tsp. salt
2 cloves garlic, cut in half
8 parsley sprigs
2 bay leaves
2 fresh thyme sprigs, or
1 tsp. dry thyme
2 stems fresh tarragon, or 1/2 tsp.
dry tarragon
3 whole black peppercorns

Peel and cube carrots, onions and celery. In a stockpot, bring
water, wine and salt to a boil. Add remaining ingredients. Reduce
heat to a simmer. Let simmer for 1 hour. Remove from heat. Set pot
on a wire rack and let cool to room temperature. Strain with a fine-
mesh strainer. Store in a covered glass container in the refrigerator
until needed.

Makes 3 quarts.

CHEF'S TIPS

- For this recipe, I prefer to use salmon, lake trout or firm saltwater fish to keep the pieces intact. It is necessary to use a stronger-flavored fish so the fish will not be overwhelmed by the chili powder.
- For garnish, mix 1 cup sour cream with 2 tsp. chili powder. Put a dollop on top of the chili.
- Shredded Farmer's cheese sprinkled on top of the sour cream adds a nice touch.
- If you feel adventurous, add a few shrimp or scallops to the chili.

Fish Chili

1 T. olive oil
1 1/2 c. red onion, chopped into 1/2-inch pieces
2 cloves garlic, minced fine
1 c. celery, peeled, cut into 1/4-inch slices
3 c. canned diced tomatoes and juice
1 c. dry red wine
1 can butter beans, drained
1 can chili beans
2 T. chili powder
1 T. fresh cilantro, chopped fine
1 tsp. salt
1/4 tsp. black pepper
1/4 tsp. ground cinnamon
1/2 tsp. ground cumin
1/2 tsp. ground allspice
2 jalapeño peppers, stem and seeds removed, diced into
1/4-inch pieces
4 c. fish, cut into 1-inch cubes

In a heavy soup pot, heat oil until hot. Add onions, garlic and celery. Sauté until tender. Add all remaining ingredients, except fish, and simmer on low heat for 30 minutes. Add fish. Cover and cook 5 minutes on low. Serve gently, being careful not to break up fish.

Serves 8 to 10.

ANGLING TIP

Spinner baits are great for catching bass during the early morning hours, on cloudy days or after dark.

Curried Smoked Fish and Pineapple

Curried Smoked Fish and Pineapple

¼ c. olive oil
1 c. red onions, diced into ¼-inch pieces
2 cloves garlic, diced fine
2 T. flour
1 T. curry powder
½ tsp. ground turmeric
½ tsp. salt
2 c. fish stock (see recipe p. 47) or clam broth
1 c. coconut milk or piña colada mix
1 c. pineapple juice
3 c. smoked fish, bones removed
1 c. fresh pineapple cubes, cut ½ inch thick
½ c. sweet coconut, shredded
½ c. cashew pieces

In a soup pot, heat oil until hot. Add red onions and garlic and cook until onions are tender and clear. Combine flour, curry powder, turmeric and salt. Add to pot. Stir with a wooden spoon to combine well. Cook 2 minutes on low heat, stirring often, being careful not to burn. Add fish stock, coconut milk and pineapple juice and bring to a simmer. Let simmer for 10 minutes. Add fish and pineapple cubes and simmer for 10 minutes.

Serve in bowls topped with coconut and cashew pieces.

Serves 4 to 6.

CHEF'S TIPS

• For a heartier soup, shrimp and scallops can be added to this recipe.
• This recipe has a mild curry flavor. If you are a curry lover, double the amount in this recipe.

ANGLING TIP

When fishing for panfish, slip bobber rigs are great for keeping the bait at the correct depth. Perch often stay near the bottom of the lake, feeding on snails and other organisms on rocks or in the mud.

CHEF'S TIPS

• Ketchup has vinegar
and spices and, if
not overused, it
adds a nice flavor to
this soup.

Skillet Fish Soup

6 slices raw bacon, diced into $1/2$-inch pieces
1 c. onion, diced into $1/2$-inch pieces
1 c. carrots, diced into $1/2$-inch pieces
1 c. celery, diced into $1/2$-inch pieces
1 c. red pepper, diced into $1/4$-inch pieces
1 T. flour
12-oz. can beer
3 c. water
2 raw potatoes, skins on, diced into $1/2$-inch cubes
1 c. ketchup
1 tsp. dry thyme
1 tsp. dry dill
1 tsp. salt
black pepper to taste
3 c. fresh fish, cut into 2-inch cubes, skins on

In an iron skillet or Dutch oven, cook bacon until brown. Add onions, carrots, celery and peppers. Cook until onions are tender, stirring with a wooden spoon to keep from burning. Add flour and stir to pick up bacon drippings. Cook for 3 minutes. Add beer, water, potatoes, ketchup, thyme, dill, salt and pepper. Simmer soup for 20 minutes. Add fish and simmer for 5 minutes. Remove from heat. Let stand covered for 5 minutes and serve.

Serves 8 to 10.

ANGLING TIP

Choose live bait
for walleye fishing
according to season:
During summer, use
leeches or night
crawlers. In the fall,
large minnows get the
most action.

Fish Gumbo

1 lb. bacon, diced into ¼-inch pieces
1 c. flour
2 c. onion, diced into ¼-inch pieces
1 c. green onion, sliced ¼ inch thick
2 c. celery, diced into ¼-inch pieces
3 cloves garlic, minced
2 c. red and green peppers, diced into ¼-inch pieces
1 qt. clam juice
¼ c. Worcestershire sauce
2 c. fresh mushrooms, sliced ¼ inch thick
2 tsp. dry thyme, or 1 T. fresh thyme
1 tsp. dry basil, or 1 T. fresh basil
1 tsp. dry oregano, or 1 T. fresh oregano
2 tsp. filé powder
1 tsp. salt
½ tsp. black pepper
3 c. diced stewed tomatoes and juice
2 jalapeño peppers, seeds removed, diced
2 c. okra, fresh or frozen, cut into ¼-inch slices
1 qt. chicken stock (see recipe p. 47)
4 smoked pork chops
4 c. cooked long-grain rice (see recipe p. 206)
3 c. catfish fillets, cut into 1½- to 2-inch pieces

A large soup pot is needed for this recipe. Dice 1 pound bacon into small pieces. Cook in pot on medium heat until brown. Remove bacon with a skimmer and place in a bowl. Add flour to the pot and stir with a wooden spoon on low heat for 10 minutes until flour and fat are browned. Do not burn as this will give the flour a bitter flavor.

Add onions, celery, garlic and peppers. Cook for 5 minutes on medium heat. Add clam juice and Worcestershire sauce and stir well to make a smooth sauce. Add mushrooms, spices, tomatoes and juice, bacon, jalapeño peppers and okra. Stir to combine. Add chicken stock and smoked pork chops. By now the pot is getting very full. Simmer on low heat for 1 hour, being careful not to boil. Stir very gently from time to time to keep ingredients from sticking to bottom of pot.

Just before serving, add fish fillets to soup. Cover and simmer for 5 minutes. Remove from heat and let steep for 5 minutes to allow flavors to fuse. In large soup bowls, place ½ cup rice and fill bowls with fish, vegetables, pork chops and broth.

Serves 8 to 10.

CHEF'S TIPS

- This recipe has many ingredients. I still find this soup one of the most fun to make, serve and enjoy.
- This recipe makes enough for leftover soup. The soup tastes better every day you keep it. It's important each time you reheat the soup to add and simmer fresh fillets.
- Pork may separate from the bones when simmering, so be careful not to serve sharp bones when you dish the soup.

ANGLING TIP

Lake trout tend to live in deeper water. Use lead-core line or down riggers to get your bait deep enough.

- This is a great soup for the kids.
- Panfish fillets are the best fish choice for this recipe.
- If you don't have Szechuan peppercorns, use black or white peppercorns.
- You may also add a few shrimp, scallops or oysters with the fillets.
- The reason for adding eggs through a strainer with the liquid moving is to keep the eggs from forming large lumps. Eggs should look wispy in the soup.

Lemon Egg Drop and Ginger Fish Soup

zest of 1 small lemon
$\frac{1}{2}$ c. dry white wine
1 c. clam broth
3 c. chicken stock (see recipe p. 47)
2 cloves garlic, minced fine
1 T. fresh ginger, peeled, diced into $\frac{1}{4}$-inch pieces
$\frac{1}{2}$ c. green onion, sliced $\frac{1}{4}$ inch thick
2 c. fresh mushrooms, sliced $\frac{1}{4}$ inch thick
6 Szechuan peppercorns
4 eggs
1 T. soy sauce
3 c. fish fillets
2 c. fresh spinach leaves, whole

With a sharp potato peeler, remove the yellow skin from a lemon in one piece. To avoid a bitter flavor, remove excess white membrane from inside of skin.

In a soup pot, combine white wine, clam broth, chicken stock, garlic and ginger. Bring to a full boil. Let boil vigorously for 5 minutes. Reduce heat. Add onions, mushrooms, lemon zest and peppercorns. Simmer for 10 minutes.

Break eggs into a bowl. Add soy sauce. Whisk to a smooth liquid. Bring soup back to a boil. Add eggs through a colander while stirring broth. Remove from heat. Add fish and spinach leaves. Cover and let steep for 5 minutes. Check fish for doneness. Serve in large soup bowls.

Serves 4 to 6.

**Lemon Egg Drop and
Ginger Fish Soup**

ANGLING TIP

Northern pike thrive in cool water. The best times to fish for pike are late spring and early summer, late summer and early fall, and in winter just after ice forms on the lakes.

Fish Bisque

4 lbs. fish bones, heads and skins
1 c. onion, cut into 1/2-inch cubes
1 c. celery, peeled and cut into 1/2-inch cubes
2 c. dry white wine
4 cloves
1 gallon cold water
2 c. Granny Smith apples, peeled and cut into 1-inch pieces

1 c. carrots, cut into 1/4-inch rounds
2 whole cloves garlic
1 c. tomato puree
1 c. roux (see recipe p. 180)
2 c. heavy cream
1 T. fresh cilantro, minced fine
3 c. boneless fish fillets, cut into 1/2-inch cubes
unsweetened whipped cream

Fillet fish. Save fish bones, heads and skins. Remove and discard entrails. Rinse off fish bones, heads and skins. Set fish fillets aside and refrigerate. Place fish bones in a cheesecloth or white cotton dish towel. Do not tie too tightly as circulation is needed to extract the flavor.

Place bone bag in a large stockpot with all remaining stock base ingredients and simmer on medium heat for 1 hour. Remove bone bag, letting all liquid drain into stockpot. Strain remaining liquid into a clean pot. While vegetables are hot, put in blender and puree. Set aside. Place pot back on heat. Bring liquid to a slow boil, reducing by half the volume. Strain again and put into a clean pot; boil until 1 quart of liquid remains.

To make soup, add tomato puree to reduced stock. Whisk roux into soup through a china cap or strainer to keep soup from lumping. Let simmer for 10 minutes, stirring to keep off bottom. In a bowl, combine cream and 1 cup hot liquid to temper. Whisk until smooth and add cream mixture to soup base. Whisk smooth. Add reserved vegetable puree. Soup should be thick and without lumps. If the soup is too thick, add a little warm milk.

Season with salt and black pepper to taste. Add cilantro and fish. Simmer 3 minutes. Cover pot and remove from heat. Let steep for 5 minutes. Serve in warm bowls and top with a large dollop of unsweetened whipped cream.

Serves 4 to 6.

Fish Stock

5 lbs. fish bones, skin and heads
1 c. carrots, cut into 1/4-inch slices
2 c. whole white onion, cut into 1/4-inch slices
1 c. fresh fennel root, cut into 1/4-inch slices
2 c. celery, cut into 1/4-inch slices
1 c. mushroom caps, cut into 1/4-inch slices
2 tsp. vegetable oil
1 sachet bag (see recipe p. 182)
2 c. dry white wine
5 qts. cold water

Fillet fish and store for future use. Save fish bones, skins with scales on and head. Remove eyes and gills and discard. Remove entrails and discard. Wash fish bones, skins and heads.

Peel carrots and clean onions, fennel, celery and mushrooms. Slice all vegetables 1/4 inch thick. In a stockpot, heat oil. Add vegetables and cook on medium heat for 7 minutes. Add fish parts, sachet bag, white wine and ice-cold water. Heat to a simmer. Water should just barely bubble. Skim off foam. Gently stir with a wooden spoon. Make sure nothing is stuck to the bottom of the pot. Simmer on low heat to reduce liquid volume by half. Remove foam from the top with a ladle often. Strain liquid through a fine strainer. Strain a second time through doubled cheesecloth or a cotton dish towel.

Makes 2 quarts.

CHEF'S TIPS

- If it were up to me, I would pass a law stating "Every fish head, as well as all skin and bones, must be used for stock."
- Fish bones are soft and, if simmered at too high a heat or for too long, they will break down and make the stock bitter and cloudy.

Chicken Stock

3 1/2 lbs. chicken wings, or 1 small stewing hen, cut up
2 c. diced onion
1 1/2 c. diced celery
1 1/2 c. diced carrots
4 qts. water
1 sachet bag (see recipe p. 182)

Wash chicken. Place all ingredients in a large soup pot and simmer on low heat for 3 1/2 hours, skimming off fat and foam from time to time. Remove from heat and strain.

Put only the liquid back in the pot and return to a fast boil until liquid has been reduced by half. Skim off fat, strain, cool and store.

Makes 4 quarts.

CHEF'S TIPS

- Remove meat from the bones and use for sandwiches and salads.

Tomato, Artichoke Hearts and White Bean Fish Soup

Tomato, Artichoke Hearts and White Bean Fish Soup

1 T. light-colored olive oil
2 whole cloves garlic
8 whole shallots
1 c. celery, cut into 1/2-inch cubes
1 c. dry white beans
1 c. dry red wine
1 qt. stewed whole tomatoes and liquid
1 qt. chicken stock (see recipe p. 47)
2 cans artichoke hearts, drained
2 T. balsamic vinegar
2 T. fresh cilantro, chopped coarse
12 panfish fillets or 3 c. fish fillets, cut into 2-inch squares
1 tsp. kosher salt
1/4 tsp. black pepper
1/2 c. shredded fresh Parmesan cheese

In a soup pot, heat olive oil. Add garlic, shallots and celery and sauté until garlic turns golden brown. Add beans and mix gently. Be careful not to break up whole shallots. Sauté until dry beans are hot. Add red wine, tomatoes and chicken stock. Reduce heat and simmer, uncovered, until beans are tender (about 45 minutes to 1 hour). If liquid starts to evaporate, add warm water to keep liquid level. Add artichoke hearts, balsamic vinegar and fresh cilantro. Gently stir to combine. Add fish. Cover and simmer 5 minutes on low heat.

Adjust seasoning with kosher salt and black pepper to taste. Serve in soup mugs. Top with freshly shredded Parmesan cheese.

Serves 8 to 10.

CHEF'S TIPS

- Black beans can be used in this recipe.
- For added color, just before serving add 1 tablespoon frozen green peas in the bottom of each soup mug.
- Shellfish and shrimp can be added with the fish fillets.
- Light-colored olive oil has less flavor than darker-colored olive oil.

CHEF'S TIPS

- This is my favorite chowder. It is a must to use salt pork and Campbell's tomato soup. The flavors are just right and there are no substitutions for these ingredients. If you do not have them, do not make this recipe.
- Thanks to the Jansson Family for this recipe.

Jansson's Fish Chowder

1 c. salt pork, diced into ¼-inch pieces
2 c. onion, diced into ¼-inch pieces
1 c. celery, diced into ¼-inch pieces
1 c. carrots, diced into ¼-inch pieces
2 cloves garlic, minced fine
1 T. fresh thyme
¼ tsp. black pepper, freshly grated
1 qt. clam broth
3 cans Campbell's tomato soup
3 c. red potatoes, skins on, cut into ½-inch cubes
4 c. boneless fish fillets, cut into 2-inch pieces

In a heavy stockpot, render salt pork to light brown. Add onions, celery, carrots and garlic. Cook until onions are transparent. Stir with a wooden spoon to keep from burning. Add thyme, black pepper and clam broth. Simmer for 30 minutes. Add tomato soup and potatoes. Simmer until potatoes are tender, about 20 minutes. Add fish pieces and simmer 5 minutes. Remove from heat. Cover and let steep for 10 minutes. Adjust seasonings to taste and serve.

Serves 6.

CHEF'S TIPS

- If shallots are not available, red onions work.
- If using fresh oysters, strain the liquid and rinse oysters in cold water to remove sand and dirt. Be very careful that oysters are fresh and from an approved location and vendor.

Panfish and Oyster Stew

3 c. crappies, cut into 1-inch cubes
2 T. butter
2 T. shallots, diced fine
¼ c. seasoned flour (see recipe p. 181)
¼ c. dry sherry
2 c. canned oysters and liquid
½ tsp. Worcestershire sauce
½ c. heavy cream
1 c. half-and-half
1 tsp. chopped fresh parsley
freshly cracked black pepper to taste

Fillet crappies. In a soup pot, heat butter to a fast bubble. Add shallots and sauté until tender. Dredge fish in seasoned flour and shake off excess flour. Place fish in butter and sauté no longer than 20 secaonds on each side. Add sherry, oysters and liquid and Worcestershire sauce. Bring liquid to a low boil. Reduce heat and simmer for 2 minutes.

Place heavy cream and half-and-half in a bowl. With a ladle, remove some of the hot liquid from the pot and add to the cream mixture to make cream warm. Add warm cream to the stew. Return stew to simmer. Gently place stew in bowls and top with parsley and black pepper. Serve with oyster crackers.

Serves 4.

- It is important to combine cream mixture with the base the way I suggested so stew doesn't curdle. The heavy cream also gives the right consistency and thickens the stew.

NOTES

You're in My Spot

After several days of cajoling, I convinced my Alaskan outfitter to return me to the remote silver salmon hole that had been hot two days prior. I had "shared" my bounty with a bear and had to promise that I would be more careful this time.

The fishing was challenging. The river was about 100 feet wide and running very fast. The bank was steep with only a foot of gravelly shoreline. When I caught a fish, I slid down the bank, fought the fish until it tired, then released it and climbed back up the bank.

Then, the big one hit. After a long, hard fight, I decided to stay on top of the bank and hoist the trophy fish up to where I was standing. With one monstrous pull, the fish became airborne and started unraveling itself from the line. With a bang that sounded like gunshot, the fish spit out the lure and swam away. At the same instant, I felt a sharp pain in my left index finger and saw the 2-ounce spoon with razor sharp hooks stuck in my finger. My finger quickly became numb from the impact.

I gently tried to remove the hook. No luck. I gave it a hard jerk. No success. I took my fishing needle nosed pliers, tucked my arm between my knees and pulled as hard as I could. Nothing.

My pain receptors came back to life and my finger started throbbing. I slid down the bank, sank my hand into the frigid water waited for the pain to dull. Then I stood on my impaled hand and pulled on the lure with all of my might until the hooks finally came loose. I looked down expecting to see blood and gore. Much to my disappointment, there was just small pinhole on the side of my finger.

Since the outfitter was not returning for several hours I continued fishing, this time from the narrow shoreline. As I cast the line, I heard what sounded at first like a bumble bee, then like a low flying plane. I hooked a large salmon and as I fought to land the fish a man in a fishing boat approached, sped up, zipped over and sliced through my line. The lunker swam away.

I was dumbfounded and temporarily at a loss for words. Then the man in the boat shouted, " You're in my spot!" I shouted, "What did you say?" He repeated, " You're in my *%!# spot."

There I was, in the far reaches of Alaska, on a narrow point in a river and this man came from out of nowhere and challenged me because I was in "his spot." This was over the top.

With all of the tact of a cranky chef and ex-submariner, I invited him to continue the conversation on shore. He declined but as he motored off, he wished me a "special" good night and signaled with some "friendly" hand gestures.

Sometimes when the weather changes my finger aches, but I still smile when I think of that day.

Salads, Sandwiches & Wraps

Day's-End Camp
Fish Salad

Day's-End Camp Fish Salad

8 strips bacon, cut into quarters
1 T. butter
1 c. onion, sliced 1/4 inch thick
4 medium fish fillets, 6 to 8 oz. each, or 8 small fillets
1/2 c. seasoned flour (see recipe p. 181)
2 c. cooked potatoes, sliced 1/4 inch thick
1/2 tsp. salt
1/8 tsp. black pepper

2 heads iceberg lettuce
1 peeled cucumber, cut into 1/4-inch cubes
2 tomatoes, cut into 1/2-inch cubes
1/2 c. blue cheese crumbles
8 to 10 crackers, broken into pieces
red French salad dressing, as needed
ranch salad dressing, as needed

In a large skillet, cook bacon until brown and crisp. Remove with a slotted spoon and set aside. Add butter and onions to skillet and cook until tender. Dredge fillets in seasoned flour and place in skillet, skin side down. Cook until light brown on both sides. Place fillets on top of cooked onions. Add potatoes, salt and pepper. Sauté until potatoes are hot. Split heads of iceberg lettuce on 4 plates. Top with potatoes, onions, fish, cucumber, tomato, bacon pieces, blue cheese and broken crackers. Serve each salad with 2 tablespoons French dressing and 2 tablespoons Ranch dressing.

Serves 4.

Panfish Tomato Polonaise

2 c. fresh whole wheat bread crumbs (see recipe p. 154)
2 hard-cooked eggs, diced into 1/4-inch cubes
1 1/2 T. fresh basil, chopped fine
1/4 tsp. black pepper

1 tsp. Hungarian paprika
1/2 c. melted butter
4 jumbo tomatoes
12 skinless panfish fillets
4 large hard rolls

Preheat oven to 350°.

To make polonaise mixture, place bread crumbs, diced eggs, chopped basil, pepper, paprika and butter in a medium-sized bowl. Toss to combine well.

Remove stem end from tomato and slice into 4 thick slices. Lay flat keeping slices in order. Top the bottom three tomato slices with 1 tablespoon of polonaise mix on each slice.

Place a fish fillet on top of each of the 3 polonaise-covered tomato slices and stack up with the last slice stem end up. Put a large pick or skewer down through the center.

Place stacked tomatoes in a baking pan and bake at 350° for 30 minutes. When fish is done, remove stacked tomatoes to a grilled hard roll. Serve liquid on the side in ramekins and enjoy.

Serves 4.

CHEF'S TIPS

- At the end of the day in camp, spending a short time to prepare and cook food in only one skillet is appealing to me.

- A soft tortilla on the bottom of the salad makes great eating and easy dish cleaning.

- This is a great dinner at home. I add avocados, cheese, sunflower seeds, cottage cheese, chopped dill pickles, hot cherry peppers or a cob or two of fresh sweet corn.

CHEF'S TIPS

- Use a small baking pan (8 inches x 8 inches) to keep the tomatoes from toppling over.

CHEF'S TIPS

• If the mix is too loose, the patties will flatten out when cooking. If the mix is too firm, the patties will crack and be dry.

Fish Burgers

2 T. butter
1/2 c. green onion, cut into 1/4-inch slices
1 c. celery, peeled and diced into 1/4-inch cubes
1 tsp. kosher salt
1/4 tsp. black pepper
1 T. fresh thyme leaves, or 1 tsp. dry thyme
1 T. horseradish, squeezed dry
2 tsp. Worcestershire sauce
4 c. boneless fish fillets, cut into 1/4-inch cubes
2 eggs, beaten until frothy
1 c. fresh whole wheat bread crumbs (see recipe p. 181)
1/2 c. tartar horseradish

Preheat oven to 350°.

In a skillet, heat 1 T. butter to a fast bubble. Add onions and celery. Cook until celery is light green and tender, about 1 to 2 minutes. Place in a large mixing bowl. Let cool for 10 minutes. Add salt, pepper, thyme, horseradish, Worcestershire sauce, fish and eggs. Combine well. Gently stir to make a paste. Sprinkle bread crumbs on top.

Combine by hand to make a firm mixture. If mixture is too loose, add more bread crumbs a few at a time. To make fish patties, fill a coffee cup with mixture. Press firm and place patty in a pan coated with seasoned flour. Roll fish patty in flour and form into desired shape. Place in refrigerator until chilled and firm.

Place a skillet on stove over medium heat. Put in remaining 1 tablespoon butter and heat. Gently add patties. Do not overcrowd. Cook until bottoms are golden brown. Turn with a wide spatula and brown the other side. Transfer patties to a cookie sheet and bake in a 350° oven for 10 minutes, or until patties are hot and firm all the way through. Serve on a roll with your favorite cheese and tartar horseradish.

Serves 4.

Wonton Fish Wraps

1 tsp. peanut oil
1 T. red onion, cut into ¼-inch cubes
1 c. Napa or red cabbage, shredded
2 tsp. white vinegar
1 tsp. soy sauce
1 tsp. fresh ginger, minced fine
2 tsp. fresh cilantro leaves, chopped medium
2 green onions, sliced ¼ inch thick
1 c. fish, diced into ¼-inch cubes
1 tsp. cornstarch
⅛ tsp. black pepper
20 to 30 wonton skins, 4 inches square
2 egg whites, beaten to a froth

Heat a small skillet and add peanut oil. Add onion and cook until tender. Do not brown. Add Napa cabbage and white vinegar. Cover and remove from heat. Let steep for 10 minutes. Remove cover and place onion/cabbage mixture in a strainer. Collect liquid and return liquid to pan. Add soy sauce, fresh ginger and cilantro. Bring to a boil. Cook down liquid until it is one-half the original volume. Remove from heat. Add green onions.

Place fish cubes with cornstarch and black pepper in a bowl and toss. Add fish cubes and cabbage/onion mixture to green onion liquid. Let cool. Form into small, tight balls. Lay wonton skin out flat on a cutting board. Brush lightly with egg whites. Place a ball in center. Fold one corner over the opposite to make a triangle. Press the air out and seal edges. Dip one of the points in egg whites and pinch with the opposite point. Place the wonton on a floured baking pan and cover with a clean dish towel. Repeat filling skins until all filling is used.

Heat oil in an electric frying pan to 375°. Fry wontons until golden brown and crisp. Remove to a paper-towel-lined bowl and serve.

To use in soup, simmer in chicken stock until wontons float to the top. Serve.

Serves 4 to 6.

CHEF'S TIPS

- If you wish to dress up the salad, add fresh pear or orange slices. Mandarin orange slices may also be added. Any trout or salmon fillet can be used in this recipe.
- I am an anchovy fan, so I add 2 fillets per salad.
- The riper and bigger the tomato, the better. Yellow tomatoes are very good as well.

Beefsteak Tomato and Fish Caesar Salad

1 head romaine lettuce
4 yellow jalapeño peppers
3 large, ripe beefsteak tomatoes
1/4 c. olive oil
4 small cloves garlic, whole
4 6- to 8-oz. fish fillets
1/2 c. seasoned flour (see recipe p. 181)
1 1/2 c. French bread, cut into 1/2-inch cubes
1/4 tsp. black pepper
1/2 c. grated Parmesan cheese
2 T. capers
lemon juice, freshly squeezed
2 c. Caesar dressing (see recipe p. 188)

Clean and remove ribs from Romaine keeping leaves in one piece. Wash, dry and chill. Cut peppers in half the long way. Remove stems, seeds and white membranes. Wash. Remove stems and cut tomatoes in 1/2-inch slices.

Heat olive oil and whole garlic in skillet. Dredge fillets and peppers in seasoned flour. Shake off excess. Fry fillets and peppers until golden brown on both sides. Remove fish and garlic to a plate. Keep warm in a 250° oven.

Add bread cubes to hot oil. Toss to keep from sticking and sauté until golden brown. Remove to a paper-towel-lined bowl. Place tomato slices in pan on low heat. Heat through.

On 4 large, chilled dinner plates place 3 to 4 romaine leaves. Top with 3 hot tomato slices, 2 pepper halves and sprinkle with black pepper. Place fish fillets on top of tomato slices. Shake Parmesan cheese over top of fillets. Top cheese with capers. Splash with fresh lemon juice and serve with Caesar dressing.

Serves 4.

Smoked Fish, Pear, Stilton and Pecan Salad

2 Bartlett pears
$1/2$ c. fresh-squeezed
orange juice
$1/2$ c. raspberry vinaigrette
1 c. fennel root, cut into
$1/4$-inch cubes

$1/2$ c. pecan halves
$1 1/2$ tsp. brown sugar
$1/4$ tsp. Spanish paprika
2 c. smoked trout
6 c. fresh lettuce greens
$1/2$ c. Stilton cheese, crumbled

Cut pears in quarters. Lay quarters on a side and remove core seeds by cutting at a 45° angle. Slice each quarter into 4 slices and place in a bowl with orange juice and raspberry vinaigrette.

Cut fennel root in quarters and remove core. Dice into pieces and place in a clean bowl. Add pecan halves. In another bowl, combine brown sugar and paprika. With a fork, remove trout flesh from skin. Pick out all small bones.

Wash greens in cold water and let drain in a colander. Evenly place greens in 4 chilled salad bowls. In a large bowl, toss fish, fennel root, pecans and Stilton cheese. Sprinkle evenly over the four salads. Decorate each salad with 8 pear slices. Sprinkle brown sugar mixture evenly over all pears. Strain orange raspberry vinaigrette and serve in a dressing boat.

Serves 4.

CHEF'S TIPS

- All smoked fish and gravlax work in this recipe.
- Yellow apples can be substituted for pears.

- If you have leftover fried or baked fish, remove excess breading before using here.
- Prior to dicing the celery, peel it with a potato peeler to remove the celery strings.

Fish Salad Tulips

2 c. cold cooked fish
2 hard-cooked eggs, chopped
1 tsp. fresh dill weed, chopped
1/2 cup mayonnaise
1/4 c. sour cream
1 tsp. lemon juice
1 tsp. Worcestershire sauce
2 tsp. sugar
pinch of salt and white pepper
1/2 c. peeled celery, diced into 1/4-inch pieces
12 tulips
1 head leaf lettuce

To make cold fish, poach boneless, skinless fillets in fish or chicken stock for 8 minutes. Cool in refrigerator. Dice cooked fish into large pieces. Be sure to remove bones.

Chop hard-cooked eggs into coarse pieces. In a bowl, combine dill, mayonnaise, sour cream, lemon juice, Worcestershire sauce, sugar, salt and pepper. Mix well. Peel celery with a potato peeler and dice into 1/4-inch pieces. Add eggs, celery and fish to mayonnaise base. Combine gently.

Pick tulips and remove pistils and stems. Place tulips in cold, salted water. Let sit for 5 minutes. Remove tulips and gently shake dry. On 4 plates place 1/4 head of leaf lettuce, place 3 tulips on top and fill each with fish salad. Serve with a sweet pickle, piece of melon and soft roll.

Serves 4.

Fish Salad Tulips

- Nasturtiums have a mild and peppery taste. Dandelions are pungent, so be conservative when adding them to the salad.
- Make sure dandelions are free from all lawn chemicals.

ANGLING TIP

When fishing for bass during periods of high fishing pressure, try switching your tactics to a finesse system. Down sizing your tackle and working it with a light touch can often bring on a strike when more traditional approaches fail. A 4-inch plastic worm, rigged weedless and with no weight, flipped toward a bed and allowed to slowly drift into a fish's "strike zone" can bring great success.

Dandelion and Nasturtium Fish Salad

8 dandelion flowers
18 nasturtium leaves (small and tender)
2 qts. water
2 tsp. salt
1 head red leaf lettuce
2 tsp. butter
1 T. shallots
2 c. fish fillets, cut into 1/2-inch cubes
1 pt. bay scallops

1 c. seasoned flour (see recipe p. 181)
1 c. scallop liquid
1/2 c. dry white wine
1/4 c. heavy cream
1 tsp. Worcestershire sauce
1 tsp. cornstarch
1/8 tsp. black pepper
2 hard-cooked eggs, diced into 1/4-inch cubes

Pick newly budded dandelion flowers. Pick the small, tender nasturtium leaves. In a large bowl, put 2 teaspoons salt in 2 quarts cold water. Add flowers and leaves. Plunge greens up and down to remove dirt and insects. Lift greens from water. Place in a colander in the refrigerator to chill. Toss lettuce in clean water the same way. Remove and store in refrigerator.

Heat a skillet with butter until it starts to bubble. Add shallots and cook until clear and tender. Toss fish fillets and scallops in seasoned flour. Shake off excess flour. Add to skillet. Sauté for 1 minute. Reduce heat to medium. Gently shake pan to keep food from sticking. Turn all pieces. Combine scallop liquid, white wine, cream, Worcestershire sauce, cornstarch and pepper; add to pan. Gently stir with a wooden spoon until sauce is thick and shiny, about 3 to 4 minutes.

Combine red lettuce and nasturtium leaves. Place equal amounts on 4 chilled dinner plates. Top with fish, scallops and sauce. With a sharp scissors, cut dandelion petals over salad for color. Sprinkle eggs around the edge of the salad on plate.

Serves 4.

Lemon, Berries and Fish Salad

2 c. cold fish pieces
½ c. seasoned flour
(see recipe p. 181)
1 T. clarified butter
(see recipe p. 189)
1 c. lemon yogurt
½ tsp. lemon zest, grated fine
1 tsp. lemon juice
¼ c. mayonnaise

¼ c. sour cream
1 T. currant jelly
½ c. celery, sliced ¼-inch thick
4 heads Boston lettuce
1½ c. fresh or frozen
blueberries
2 c. fresh strawberries,
cut in half
1 lime, cut into 4 wedges

Use boneless, skinless firm fish fillets. Cut into 1-inch cubes. Roll in seasoned flour. Shake off excess. Heat clarified butter in skillet. Add fish cubes and sauté to light brown on all sides. Remove to a rack to cool.

In a bowl, combine yogurt, lemon zest, lemon juice, mayonnaise, sour cream and currant jelly. Add celery and fish. Fold together gently. Cover and chill for 1 hour. Wash and remove cores from lettuce. Shake dry. Place a head in the centers of 4 chilled dinner plates. With a large spoon, place fish mixture in 4 even portions in each lettuce head. Top with blueberries and strawberries. Garnish with a lime wedge.

Serves 4.

CHEF'S TIPS

• Any berry in season can be used.
• Add cold shrimp or scallops as part of the fish portion of the recipe.
• When adding frozen blueberries to the mix, thaw and drain them first. Otherwise they will bleed and turn everything in the salad purple.

Achilles' Greek Fish Salad

3 c. spinach leaves, stemmed
1 head romaine lettuce
1 c. seasoned flour
(see recipe p. 181)
2 tsp. dry oregano
2 T. olive oil
3 cloves garlic, whole

12 panfish fillets with
scales and skins
1 T. fresh lemon juice
¼ c. apple juice
¼ tsp. lemon zest, grated
½ c. feta cheese
8 kalamata olives
16 anchovy fillets

Wash and clean spinach. Remove stems. Wash and remove ribs from romaine lettuce. Tear greens into bite-sized pieces. Place greens in a plastic bag in refrigerator until crisp, at least 1 hour.

Combine seasoned flour and oregano and put in pie pan. In a skillet, heat olive oil and garlic. Dredge fillets in seasoned flour. Lightly shake off excess. Lay skin side down in skillet. Cook fish fillets until golden brown. Turn and repeat. Place fish and garlic in a paper-towel-lined bowl. Add 1 teaspoon oregano/flour mixture to oil in skillet. Stir with a wooden spoon to make a smooth sauce. Bring to a bubble. Add lemon juice, apple juice and zest. Remove from heat.

Place even amounts of greens on 4 chilled plates. Place 3 fish fillets on each salad. Evenly pour lemon sauce over fish. Sprinkle with crumbled feta cheese. Garnish with kalamata olives and anchovy fillets.

Serves 4.

CHEF'S TIPS

•Be careful not to burn whole garlic cloves. If they start to get too brown, remove them from the oil or they will be the Achilles' heel in your salad.

Fish BLT Triple Deckers

Fish BLT Triple Deckers

4 6- to 8-oz. fish fillets or boneless steaks
2 avocados, peeled and sliced ½ inch thick
1 T. fresh lemon juice
1 c. tartar sauce (see recipe p. 171)
1 T. capers
2 large fresh tomatoes, cut into ½-inch-thick slices
1 tsp. kosher salt
black pepper to taste
12 slices sourdough bread
1 head leaf lettuce
8 strips bacon, crisp-cooked

Grill or fry fish fillets. Place avocados in a bowl with lemon juice. Add tartar sauce and capers. Remove stems and slice tomatoes. Sprinkle with kosher salt and grind fresh black pepper to taste over the top of tomatoes. Toast bread golden brown and lay bread slices on a cotton towel in lines 3 slices tall.

To make triple decker: Spread each bread slice with a generous amount of tartar sauce. On two slices place a leaf of lettuce. Top one lettuce leaf with 2 tomato slices and 2 pieces of bacon. Top the other lettuce leaf with fish and avocado slices.

Now the fun part. Top the bacon/lettuce/tomato piece with the slice that has tartar sauce on it (sauce side down). Spread dry side with more tartar sauce and add a lettuce leaf. Turn fish slice over top of middle slice to make the 3rd deck. Put 2 long picks in the sandwich to fasten. Cut in half. Serve with a kosher dill pickle.

Serves 4.

- This sandwich is a whopper to see, but even more fun to eat.
- The way to keep all 3 decks together is to spread sauce on the dry side of the middle slice of bread.
- Crisp iceberg lettuce may be used in place of leaf lettuce.
- If you are not a bacon lover, use turkey or corned beef.

CHEF'S TIPS

• "Grinder" is another name for submarine sandwich.

• Any boneless fish steak or fillet can be used in the recipe. I prefer yellowfin tuna steaks.

• Panfish are too tender and will break up on grill.

• For another version, deep fry the fish.

• Use your imagination when building this sandwich. Incorporate fresh-grilled fruits or vegetables, capers or hot peppers, to name a few.

• Good luck eating it! This is a two-handed sandwich, to be sure.

Grilled Fish and Vegetable Grinders

1 c. mayonnaise
1 T. lemon juice
1 T. Chef John's fish rub (see recipe p. 183)
1 tsp. spicy mustard
4 6- to 8-oz. fish steaks
1/2 c. vegetable oil
2/3 c. barbeque sauce
2 large red peppers, seeded and cut into 3 wedges
3 large carrots, cut into 1/4-inch-thick slices the long way
2 large red onions, cut into 1/2-inch-thick slices
2 large ripe tomatoes, cut into 1/2-inch-thick slices
3 large baking potatoes, cut into 1/2-inch-thick slices the long way
1 c. tartar sauce (see recipe p. 171)
1 tsp. garlic salt
1/4 tsp. black pepper
1 c. Muenster cheese, shredded
12- to 14-inch loaf of French or Italian bread
1 head iceberg lettuce
1 c. black olive slices

Place mayonnaise, lemon juice, fish rub and mustard in a 1-gallon sealable plastic bag. Shake to combine. Add fish steaks and shake gently to coat steaks. Refrigerate 1 to 2 hours. Place vegetable oil and barbeque sauce in a cake pan. Dip cut vegetables in barbeque-flavored oil and place on a hot grill. Remove fish from bag, leaving a thick coat of mayonnaise mixture on fillets. Add to grill. Grill vegetables and fish until golden brown. Turn and grill until tender.

Combine tartar sauce, garlic salt, black pepper and shredded Muenster cheese. Cut French loaf in half the long way. Spread each half loaf with 1/2 c. tartar sauce mixture. Lay bread halves on a platter. Top the bottom half with grilled potatoes. Brush with barbeque-flavored oil. Add red pepper wedges, lettuce leaves, black olive slices, fish steaks, grilled tomato, onion and carrot slices. Brush with barbeque-flavored oil.

Turn top slice quickly onto bottom slice. Cut into 4 portions. Fasten each portion with long frill picks.

Serves 4.

English Fish and Chips Sandwich

8 4-oz. firm, white boneless,
skinless fish fillets
2 c. ice cubes
1 tsp. salt
1 qt. cold water
2 c. vegetable oil
1 c. seasoned flour
(see recipe p. 181)
6 to 8 c. french fries
8 slices English muffin bread,
toasted

¼ c. malt vinegar
kosher salt to taste
black pepper to taste

Batter
1 egg yolk
¼ c. beer
¼ c. cold water
¼ c. milk
1 c. all-purpose flour
2 egg whites

Cut boneless fillets into 4-inch squares. Place in a bowl with ice, salt and cold water to make fish firm.

To make batter, place egg yolk, beer, water and milk in a bowl. Whisk to combine. Slowly whisk in flour. Refrigerate for 15 to 20 minutes. In a small clean bowl, beat egg whites stiff. Gently and thoroughly fold egg whites into batter.

In deep fryer, heat vegetable oil to 375°. Remove fish from salt water and pat dry. Toss in seasoned flour. Shake off excess flour and dip into batter. When fillet is well coated, place in hot oil. Fry 3 to 4 pieces at a time, turning the pieces to keep them from sticking together. Fry 4 to 5 minutes, or until golden brown. Remove to paper-towel-lined bowl. Cover with paper towel to keep warm.

Fry french fries until crisp. Toast bread slices and butter them. Place 4 slices on warm plates. Top with french fries and fish. Serve with malt vinegar. Season with a generous amount of kosher salt and cracked black pepper.

Serves 4.

CHEF'S TIPS
- The British name for french fries is chips.
- They often use shark meat and traditionally serve fish and chips wrapped in a newspaper.
- To make homemade french fries, take 4 large Idaho baker potatoes, cut into strips the size of your small finger, and deep fry until golden brown.

CHEF'S TIPS

• This is an excellent
way to prepare strong-
flavored fish like bass,
bluefish or lake trout.

Fish Reubens

4 6- to 8-oz. skinless fillets
1/3 c. seasoned flour (see recipe p. 181)
1/2 c. egg wash (see recipe p. 181)
2 c. fresh pumpernickel bread crumbs (see bread crumb recipe p. 181)
1 1/2 T. clarified butter (see recipe p. 189)
1/3 c. Thousand Island dressing (see recipe p. 177)
8 slices Swiss cheese
4 c. spätzle (see recipe p. 223)
2 c. sweet kraut

Preheat oven to 375°.

Lightly coat fish fillets with seasoned flour. Dip in egg wash.
Shake off excess and coat with pumpernickel crumbs.

Heat an ovenproof skillet with clarified butter. Add fish fillets and
brown. Turn fish fillets. Remove from heat. Top each fillet with 1 T.
Thousand Island dressing and 2 pieces Swiss cheese. Place skillet in
a 375° oven for 8 to 10 minutes, until cheese turns light brown and
starts to bubble. Serve with spätzle and sweet kraut.

Serves 4.

CHEF'S TIPS

• This recipe also
works well with
all types of grilled
saltwater fish steaks
or cold leftover bone-
less fish.

• Tough guys or gals
also toss in one or
two of their favorite
hot peppers!

Popeye Fish Sandwich

4 6- to 8-oz. boneless fish
steaks
1 c. herb dressing
4 c. fresh spinach leaves,
stems removed
1 large red onion, peeled and
cut into 1/4-inch slices

2 T. vegetable oil
4 1-oz. slices dill Havarti
cheese
4 French or Italian hard rolls
1/3 c. honey mustard
4 slices pineapple rings

Place fish steaks in a large sealable plastic bag with herb dressing.
Refrigerate for 1 hour. Thoroughly wash and remove stems from fresh
spinach.

To prepare onion, lay out a triple layer of paper towels. Place onion
slices on paper towel and top with another triple-thick layer of paper
towels. With the palm of your hand, press on onion slices firmly to
squeeze out juice. Turn onion slices over and repeat.

To cook fish, heat oil in a skillet. Remove fish from herb dressing
and pan-fry golden brown on both sides.

To assemble sandwich, slice hard rolls in half. Spread both sides of
roll with honey mustard. On top half of each roll, place 1 cup spinach,
1 slice cheese and onion slices. On bottom half, place 1 piece fish and
pineapple ring. Close sandwiches and serve.

Serves 4.

Fish Reubens

CHEF'S TIPS

• Shrimp, oysters, scallops and lobster tails cut in half can be used in place of fish fillet strips.

Asian Fish Dip

Broth

1 qt. clam broth
1 c. celery, cut into ¼-inch slices
1 c. carrots, cut into ¼-inch slices
2 cloves garlic, mashed
⅓ c. soy sauce
1 T. fresh gingerroot, sliced ¼ inch thick

Batter

1 c. flour
1 c. cornstarch
½ tsp. brown sugar
⅛ tsp. white pepper
1 tsp. baking powder
1 whole egg
1 egg yolk
1 T. vegetable oil
1 T. white vinegar
1¼ c. ice-cold water

4 hard rolls
4 6- to 8-oz. boneless fish fillets
½ c. seasoned flour (see recipe p. 181)

To make broth, place all broth ingredients in a heavy saucepan and simmer on low heat for 30 minutes.

Butter and grill four hard rolls. While broth is simmering, make batter. Combine all dry batter ingredients. In a bowl, whisk egg and egg yolk until smooth. Add oil, vinegar and cold water. Whisk to combine. Add dry ingredients and slowly whisk until smooth. Refrigerate until needed.

Heat oil in a deep fryer or electric skillet to 375°. Cut fish in strips 1 inch wide and 3 to 4 inches long. Dredge in seasoned flour and shake off excess flour. Dip into batter and deep-fry at 375° for 2 to 3 minutes. When batter is golden brown remove to paper-towel-lined bowl.

Strain hot broth into bouillon cups. Place fish strips onto grilled hard rolls. On large serving plate, place one sandwich and one cup broth for dipping, a crisp dill pickle and thick ruffled potato chips.

Serves 4.

Fish Tacos

1 T. taco seasoning mix
1 c. seasoned flour (see recipe p. 181)
4 c. boneless fish, cut into 1-inch cubes
4 drops Tabasco sauce
1 c. egg wash (see recipe p. 181)
2 c. white or blue cornmeal
10 to 12 taco shells
3 c. vegetable oil

shredded lettuce
shredded cheese
diced tomatoes
diced dill pickles
sliced black olives
capers
fresh cilantro
sliced hot peppers
guacamole
sour cream

Combine taco seasoning with flour. Place in a pie pan. Dredge fish cubes in seasoned flour mixture. Add Tabasco sauce to egg wash and combine. Dip floured cubes in egg wash and roll in cornmeal to create a thick crust. Place on a cornmeal-dusted platter.

Preheat oven to 350°. Place taco shells in oven for 5 minutes to heat and crisp. Put vegetable oil in a deep fryer or electric skillet and heat to 350°. Deep-fry fish until golden brown. Remove to a paper-towel-lined bowl.

To serve, place fried fish in taco shells and fill with taco fixings.

Serves 4.

• Try adding diced chili peppers and salsa instead of the horseradish sauce.

Irish Cabbage and Potato Fish Wraps

2 red potatoes, peeled and cut in half
3 carrots, peeled and cut into 2-inch pieces
1 gallon water
1 T. salt
1 pickling spice bag (see recipe p. 183)
$\frac{1}{2}$ c. sour cream
$\frac{1}{4}$ c. red onion, diced into $\frac{1}{4}$-inch pieces
1 tsp. white vinegar
1 T. horseradish, drained
$\frac{1}{4}$ tsp. black pepper
1 head green cabbage, outside leaves removed
4 salmon fillets, $1\frac{1}{2}$ inches wide and 6 inches long
4 large flour tortillas, 10-inch diameter
4 tsp. horseradish sauce (see recipe p. 175)

Place potatoes and carrots in a pot with salted water and a pickling spice bag. Boil until potatoes and carrots are tender. With a skimmer, remove potatoes and carrots and place in a bowl. Let steam for 3 to 4 minutes. Add sour cream, diced onions, vinegar, horseradish and pepper. Mash, leaving a few small lumps for texture. Cover to keep warm.

Return water to a fast boil. Cut the core out of the cabbage at least 2 inches down. Poke a meat fork in the center of the hole. Be sure not to poke fork through the other side or leaves will not loosen. Plunge cabbage up and down in boiling water to loosen leaves. When 8 to 10 large leaves are loose, remove cabbage. Let leaves remain in water. Add fish and simmer for 5 minutes. Gently lift fish and leaves with a slotted spoon to a strainer. Remove the thick ribs from cabbage leaves. Cover to keep warm.

Lay 4 flour tortillas on a flat, clean surface. Spread potato/carrot mixture evenly over tortillas. Top with cabbage leaves and place a piece of fish in the center. Top each fish piece with 1 teaspoon horseradish sauce. Trim cabbage leaves the same size as the tortilla shells. When cabbage is trimmed, roll into a cylinder. Brush the outside with soft butter.

Serves 4.

**Irish Cabbage and Potato
Fish Wraps**

• Shrimp, oysters, scallops and soft-shelled crabs can be used in place of fish.

• Pile on your favorite trimmings. I like to add diced tomatoes, cheese and dill pickles.

ANGLING TIP

The best method for catching Chinook salmon in deep lakes is trolling with a plug or spoon. Use downriggers to get the lure down to where the fish are swimming.

Cajun Beer Batter Fillets in Kaiser Rolls

12-oz. bottle or can of beer
1 c. flour
1 c. seasoned flour (see recipe p. 181)
1 T. Cajun seasoning
8 jalapeño peppers
12 fish pieces, 2 inches long and 1 inch wide
2 c. vegetable oil
4 onion Kaiser rolls
½ c. flavored mayonnaise (see recipe p. 187)
2 c. iceberg lettuce, shredded

Place beer in a medium-sized bowl. Add flour and whisk smooth. In a pie plate, combine 1 cup seasoned flour and ½ tablespoon Cajun seasoning. Cut peppers in half and remove stem, seeds and white membranes. Moisten peppers and dredge in seasoned flour with fish pieces.

In an electric frying pan heat oil to 375°. Shake off excess flour from fillets and peppers and dip pieces in beer batter. Let excess batter drip off gently. Place fish pieces and peppers in hot oil. Cook until batter is orange-brown in color. Turn and repeat. Remove fish and pepper pieces to a bowl lined with a generous amount of paper towels. Shake the rest of the Cajun seasoning over the pieces.

Split Kaiser rolls in half, leaving one side hinged. Spread both sides with mayonnaise. Add a generous amount of shredded lettuce and stuff with fish and pepper pieces.

Serves 4.

Hoppin' Jay's Shrimp Catfish Salad

1 lb. dry black-eyed peas
1/2 c. bacon, cut into 1/4-inch pieces
2 c. onion, cut into 1/4-inch cubes
2 cloves garlic, cut into 1/4-inch slices
1 c. ham, cut into 1/2-inch cubes
3 c. chicken stock (see recipe p. 47)
2 c. clam juice
2 tsp. fresh oregano
4 drops Tabasco sauce
2 tsp. fresh thyme
1 tsp. salt
16 fresh shrimp (shells on)
2 c. catfish, cut into 1-inch cubes
1 to 2 lbs. spinach or Swiss chard leaves
4 c. cooked long-grain white rice (see recipe p. 211)

Preheat oven to 350°.

Soak peas overnight in water. Make sure water is 2 inches above peas. In a large iron skillet or Dutch oven, brown bacon. Add onions, garlic and ham. Sauté until onions are clear and tender. Add chicken stock, clam juice, oregano, Tabasco, thyme and salt. Bring to a boil. Drain peas and add to skillet.

Cover and bake in a 350° oven for 1 hour. Remove from oven. Combine well. Add shrimp and catfish. Cover and bake for 10 more minutes. Remove from oven and let steep for 15 minutes.

Place generous amount of washed salad greens on four large dinner plates. Top greens with 1 cup rice, 1 cup peas and catfish mixture and 4 shrimp.

Serves 4.

CHEF'S TIPS

• As the legend goes, if eaten on New Year's Eve this salad will bring you good luck for the new year.

CHEF'S TIPS

• If you wish to dress up the salad, add fresh pear or orange slices. Mandarin orange slices may also be added.

Crunchy Fish and Oyster Salad

¾ c. blue cornmeal
½ c. Parmesan cheese
1 c. vegetable oil
8 boneless pieces of fish, cut 1 inch wide and 3 inches long
8 fresh oysters, shucked
1 c. seasoned flour (see recipe p. 181)
1 c. egg wash (see recipe p. 181)
2 heads romaine hearts
2 T. Parmesan cheese, freshly grated
8 strips bacon, cooked crisp
black pepper to taste
½ c. vinaigrette dressing

Combine cornmeal and ½ cup cheese in a medium-sized bowl. Heat oil to 375° in an electric fry pan or skillet. Dredge fish and oysters in seasoned flour. Dip into egg wash. Shake off excess liquid. Roll in cornmeal mix. Place fish in oil.

Fry until golden brown. Remove to a paper-towel-lined bowl. Repeat process with oysters, frying a little browner than the fish.

Remove all ribs and outer leaves from Romaine lettuce. Break leaves into large pieces and place on chilled dinner plates. Place 2 pieces fish and 2 oysters on top of each salad. Top with ½ tablespoon cheese, 2 bacon strips, a generous amount of ground black pepper and your favorite vinaigrette or Caesar dressing.

Serves 4.

NOTES

_____

_____

_____

_____

_____

_____

_____

_____

_____

_____

_____

_____

_____

_____

_____

_____

_____

_____

_____

_____

_____

_____

_____

_____

_____

_____

_____

_____

_____

_____

_____

FATHER-SON FISHING TRIP

I heard the walleyes were biting in a nearby reservoir, so I called my son Carlton and set up the trip. When the time came for us leave after a good day of fishing, we stowed the gear and took off. Assuming we were heading the right direction we kept going, thinking that things might look more familiar as we neared the launch. We soon realized that we'd gone the exact opposite direction and were seven miles from where we were supposed to be.

As we turned back the sun was going down. After motoring about two miles, the engine started to sputter. Carlton looked at me with a pursed lip and said, "Stop fooling around."

Now, my son contends that I have an odd way about me, making a big deal about little things and taking the big things lightly. This turned out to be a big thing. The motor died and we were out of gas.

Carlton tried call 911 with a cell phone as daylight steadily faded. All he got was a message saying there was no service in the area.

So the stage is set: We were in the middle of the reservoir more than a mile from shore. Carlton started the bow-mount trolling motor and headed for shore. As darkness set, the shoreline lost definition. We were much farther away than we both imagined. As my son tells it, he was focused on saving our lives when he looked back to see me eating a Nut Goody bar, fishing rod in hand.

After a brief discussion about how good an idea it was to fish right then, we realized that the huge thunderhead we saw forming during the afternoon now loomed right behind us. A wall of blackness was coming with streaks of lightning hitting the water. The wind now blew hard enough to spray the tops off the newly formed whitecaps.

We put on our life jackets. Carlton had to lie on the bow of the boat to work the trolling motor without getting tossed out. The waves were nearly six feet high. I used the main motor as a tiller to quarter into the waves and keep from getting swamped.

I had Carlton tie rope from the back of the boat to the front along the gunnels. He asked me why, and the answer made him nervous: "When the boat flips, stay with the boat and grab the line."

Although we'd been giving each other grief the whole trip, we were now completely focused and working as a team. He steered toward shore as I kept us righted. After what seemed like forever we got close to a point of land. Carlton jumped into waste deep water as waves pounded the boat, hauled the boat up and tied it off as best he could. We breathed a sigh of relief, then grabbed an umbrella, seat cushions and life jackets from the boat. We spent that night under some bushes and the umbrella.

The next morning we flagged a passing boater who called a service to deliver gas to us. We arrived back at the launch as everyone was putting in for the day. One guy who recognized from the day before asked us, "How was the fishing?" Carlton and I just looked at each other and nodded vigorously. "Fishing was pretty good."

Deep-Fried & Poached

CHEF'S TIPS

- Orange, almond or vanilla extract can be used in this recipe. Be cautious when adding extracts because they are highly concentrated and a little goes a long way.
- This batter works with all seafood, vegetables and cut fresh fruit.

Lemon Tempura-Battered Fish Fillets

1 c. flour	¼ tsp. lemon extract
¼ c. cornstarch	1 c. sesame or peanut oil
pinch white pepper	8 4-oz. fish fillets
1 c. cold skim milk	½ c. seasoned flour
1 egg yolk	(see recipe p. 181)

To make tempura batter, combine flour, cornstarch and white pepper. Place skim milk, egg yolk and lemon extract in another bowl. Whisk until smooth. Add dry ingredients to the liquid and whisk to make a smooth batter. Keep batter refrigerated.

Heat oil in an electric frying pan to 350°.

Roll fish in seasoned flour and shake off excess flour. Dip fish fillets in tempura batter. Fry in oil at 350° until crisp and golden brown. Remove to an absorbent paper towel. Serve with your favorite dipping sauce or seasoning.

Serves 4.

CHEF'S TIPS

- This tried-and-true recipe can be made with many variations.
- Use different kinds of bread when making bread crumbs.
- Add your favorite hot sauce to the egg wash.
- Add your favorite spices to the flour.

Traditional Breaded Fish Fillets

8 4- to 6-oz. boneless fish fillets
1 c. seasoned flour (see recipe p. 181)
1 c. egg wash (see recipe p. 181)
2 c. fresh bread crumbs (see recipe p. 181)
1½ c. vegetable oil
2 tsp. lemon juice
tartar sauce (see recipe p. 171)

Coat fish fillets in seasoned flour. Shake off excess flour. Dip in egg wash and shake off excess. Dredge fish fillets in fresh bread crumbs. In an electric fry pan or deep fryer, heat oil to 375°. Fry fish in hot oil until brown and crisp. Remove and place on a paper-towel-lined platter. Splash with lemon juice. Serve with tartar sauce.

Serves 4.

Gingered Rum and Molasses Salmon

2 c. buttermilk
¼ c. dark rum
½ c. molasses
4 8-oz. boneless salmon pieces
¼ c. fresh ginger, cut into
1-inch pieces

2 c. seasoned flour
(see recipe p. 154)
4 c. grits (see recipe p. 224)
2 c. vegetable oil
2 tsp. fresh lime juice
2 limes, cut in half

In a glass or stainless steel bowl, combine buttermilk, rum and molasses. Add salmon and fresh ginger. Cover and refrigerate overnight.

To prepare, remove fish and dredge in seasoned flour. Place on a rack to dry for 10 minutes. Dip fish in marinade and dredge in grits. Return to rack for 3 minutes. Heat vegetable oil to 350° in an electric skillet. Add fish to oil and deep-fry until golden brown. Remove and place on a paper-towel-lined serving plate. Splash with lime juice. Serve with fresh lime halves.

Serves 4.

Poached Fish Fillets in Pineapple Salsa

2 c. pineapple salsa (see recipe p. 194)
1 c. dry red wine
8 4- to 6-oz. fish fillets, skin on
4 c. taco chips
1 fresh lime, cut into quarters

In a Dutch oven, heat pineapple salsa and red wine to a bubble. Top salsa with fish fillets. Cover pan and simmer for 3 minutes. Remove from heat. Let sit for 8 to 10 minutes. Test for doneness.

Serve 2 fish fillets topped with ½ cup salsa on a warm dinner plate. Garnish with taco chips and a large lime wedge.

Serves 4.

CHEF'S TIPS

• This recipe needs a firm fish that will hold together. Yellow-fin tuna, halibut, shark and catfish can be substituted for salmon.

CHEF'S TIPS

• It is important to place the fillets on top of the salsa so that they remain in one piece when removing from the Dutch oven.

• For extra zest, garnish with sour cream, shredded cheddar cheese, black olive slices or diced raw onions.

Fish Kiev

Fish Kiev

Butter Filling

½ lb. softened butter
2 T. shallots, minced fine
2 tsp. fresh tarragon
2 tsp. lemon juice
½ tsp. Worcestershire sauce
3 drops Tabasco sauce
¼ tsp. lemon zest
1½ T. fresh white bread crumbs (see recipe p. 181)

pinch white pepper

• • • • •

2 lbs. boneless, skinless fish, cut into 1½- to 2-inch cubes
1 c. seasoned flour (see recipe p. 181)
1 c. egg wash (see recipe p. 181)
2 to 3 c. fresh bread crumbs (see recipe p. 181)

Combine all ingredients for butter-filling mixture. Place in ice cube trays lined with plastic wrap. Fill each cube half-full. Freeze.

With a short knife, slice a pocket into each piece of fish. Leave a ¼-inch wall on 3 sides. Heat oil in a deep fryer or electric skillet to 375°.

To prepare, remove butter filling from freezer as close to assembly as possible. Stuff one pat of butter filling in each fish pocket. Roll the fish cubes in seasoned flour. Shake off excess flour. Dip in egg wash. Shake off excess. Return to flour. Coat well. Return to egg wash, then into fresh bread crumbs, pressing gently to coat. Fry in a 375° deep fryer until golden brown. Remove and serve with fresh lemon wedge.

Serves 4.

Beer-Battered Fish

6 to 8 boneless panfish fillets, or 4 to 6 2-inch fish squares
12-oz. bottle or can of beer
1 c. flour
¼ c. seasoned flour (see recipe p. 181)
1 qt. canola oil for frying

Pour beer in a bowl. Add 1 cup flour. Whisk smooth. Refrigerate until needed. Heat a deep fryer or electric skillet to 375°. Dredge fish pieces in seasoned flour and shake off excess flour. Dip in batter. Shake off excess batter. Fry in 375° oil until golden brown. Remove to a paper-towel-lined bowl. Sprinkle with your favorite seasoning.

Serves 4.

- For battered vegetables, use the same preparation with small vegetable pieces.
- For battered fruit, roll fruit in a shallow dish with 1 cup granulated sugar and 1 teaspoon ground cinnamon after frying.

CHEF'S TIPS

• The purpose of freezing the butter mixture is to keep it from liquifying when it is deep-fried.
• The process of rolling the fish cubes in flour twice is necessary to form a tight seal.
• Exercise caution when first biting into the cooked fish kiev. The butter filling is very hot!

CHEF'S TIPS

• This recipe works well because it does not contain salt. Salt would break down the frying oil, causing it to separate and burn.
• Add seasonings after frying the fish.
• Canola oil has a mild flavor and high smoke point.

• Fish fillets should not be thicker than 1/2 inch or longer than 3 inches. Larger fillets will absorb too much oil.

Crispy Coconut Fish

1 1/2 tsp. chili powder
1/4 tsp. black pepper
1/4 tsp. garlic powder
1/4 tsp. dry mustard
1 c. fresh white bread crumbs (see recipe p. 181)
1/2 c. shredded coconut
2 c. vegetable oil
12 boneless panfish fillets, skins on 1 c. seasoned flour
(see recipe p. 181)
1 c. egg wash (see recipe p. 181)
1 c. pineapple mayonnaise (see recipe p. 188)

Sift chili powder, black pepper, garlic powder and mustard into a pie plate. Combine fresh bread crumbs with shredded coconut. In an electric fry pan or deep fryer, heat oil to 375°. Dredge fish fillets in flour mixture. Shake off excess flour. Dip in egg wash. Shake off excess. Cover with coconut/bread crumb mixture. Deep fry until golden brown. Remove to a paper-towel-lined plate. Serve with pineapple mayonnaise.

Serves 4.

ANGLING TIP

When fishing for bass, surface lures are most productive in shallow water (six feet and less).

Poached Perch with Cucumber Sauce

Poaching liquid and vegetables

2 c. water
$1/2$ c. onion, cut into 3-inch-long matchsticks
$1/4$ c. carrots, cut into 3-inch-long matchsticks
$1/4$ c. celery, cut into 3-inch-long matchsticks
1 bay leaf
$1/2$ c. dry white wine
$1/2$ lemon, seeds removed
6 peppercorns
$1/4$ tsp. salt

12 boneless perch or panfish fillets
4 c. long-grain rice (see recipe p. 211)
2 c. cucumber sauce (see recipe p. 178)

Place all poaching liquid and vegetable ingredients in a medium-sized saucepan and simmer on low heat for 10 minutes. Bring to a boil. Add fish fillets. Remove from heat and cover for 8 to 10 minutes. Remove fillets very carefully with a slotted spoon.

To serve, place fish on steamed rice and top with matchstick vegetables. Place cucumber sauce in a ramekin and serve on the side.

Serves 4.

CHEF'S TIPS

- For larger fish, cut boneless fish fillets into 4-inch squares. Fish should not be over $1/2$ inch thick.

**Yellow Cornmeal and
Parmesan Catfish**

Yellow Cornmeal and Parmesan Catfish

1 c. seasoned flour (see recipe p. 181)
1 c. freshly grated Parmesan cheese
1 c. cornmeal (yellow or white)
1 T. dry parsley flakes
2 eggs
¾ c. milk
2 c. vegetable oil
¼ c. butter
4 catfish fillets, skinned and cut into 5-inch slabs
1 T. fresh lemon juice
1 tsp. seasoning of choice (Cajun, taco or lemon pepper)

Place seasoned flour in a pie pan. Mix Parmesan cheese, cornmeal and parsley flakes in another pie pan.

Combine eggs and milk in a shallow bowl. Whisk mixture to a froth. Heat oil in an electric fry pan to 375°. When oil is hot, add butter. Dredge fish in flour mixture. Shake off excess flour. Dip fish in egg wash then roll in cornmeal mixture. Shake off excess cornmeal and place fish fillets in hot oil.

Brown on one side for about 2 minutes, being careful not to overcook. Turn and cook until done. Remove from oil and place on paper-towel-lined dish.

Lightly splash with lemon juice and dust with your favorite seasoning.

Serves 4.

CHEF'S TIPS

- This is an excellent breading for deep-frying all varieties of fish fillets.
- The oil needs to be 375 degrees. If it is too hot the fish will burn. If it is too cold the fish will absorb too much oil.
- To add some spiciness, fry chili peppers after removing stems and seeds.

- This recipe is intended for lake trout, salmon, white fish, striped bass, cod and scrod. It is an excellent change after eating fried fish for a week.

- Be careful not to pour out the rice when draining off the liquid. This is difficult to do but very important.

ANGLING TIP

When choosing lures, remember that fish use hearing, smell and sight to locate food. For predator fish, hearing is most important.

Boiled Shore Lunch

8 to 10 2-inch-thick fish steaks, scaled
4 medium red potatoes, skins on
4 whole carrots, peeled
4 small red onions, peeled
4 large whole dill pickles
1 T. salt
1/2 T. fresh thyme
3 bay leaves
1/2 tsp. black pepper
3 cloves garlic, whole
1 1/2 to 2 gallons cold water
1 1/2 c. dry long-grain rice
1/2 lb. butter

First you have to catch the fish. This is the hard part. Then clean, scale and cut into fish steaks.

Place potatoes, carrots, onions, dill pickles, salt, thyme, bay leaves, pepper and garlic in a large pot with cold water. Cover and bring to a boil over hot campfire or gas grill. When water boils, add rice. Boil for 30 minutes. Add fish and boil 5 minutes. With help, remove pot from fire. Leaving the cover on, drain the liquid completely. Remove cover. Top fish with slabs of butter. Let vegetables and fish steam off. For each hungry fisherman, place a potato, onion, pickle and 2 pieces of fish on a plate. Top with butter/rice mixture.

Serves 4.

Milk-Poached Pike

1 4- to 5-lb. pike (if you are lucky enough to catch one)
2 qts. milk
2 celery stalks
2 bay leaves
6 peppercorns
2 cloves garlic
2 tsp. fresh thyme leaves
1 tsp. salt
4 whole cloves
3 pieces lemon zest, 3 inches long and 1 inch wide
½ c. roux (see recipe p. 180)
2 tsp. dry mustard

Scale both sides, belly and back of the fish. Remove insides, gills and eyes, and wash inside of fish with a vegetable brush.

Preheat oven to 375°. In a poaching or large baking pan, place fish. Cover with a damp cloth. Keep refrigerated until needed.

In a saucepot, heat milk, celery, bay leaves, peppercorns, garlic, thyme, salt and cloves. Let simmer on low heat for 10 minutes, being careful not to boil. Add lemon zest. Remove from heat. Let steep for 30 minutes.

Remove fish from refrigerator. Remove cloth. Strain stock over fish. Make sure fish is completely covered. If more liquid is needed, add cold water. Cover tightly with double-thick aluminum foil. Place in a 375° oven for 45 minutes. To test for doneness, fold back ¼ foil. Press meat with a fork. When fish is milky white and flaky but still firm, it is done. Drain liquid into a saucepot to keep warm. Keep cooked fish covered. Turn off oven. Return fish to oven until service.

In a saucepot, place 1 quart poaching milk and bring to a simmer. Thicken with a mixture of ½ cup roux and 2 teaspoons dry mustard. Whisk well. Let simmer on low heat for 10 minutes. Place in a blender for 30 seconds to make an extra-smooth sauce.

Serve pike on long serving dish. Remove skin and meat from one side of fish at a time, making sure to remove the tiny Y bones. Serve with creamy mustard sauce and a large wedge of fresh lemon.

Serves 4 to 6.

CHEF'S TIPS

- This recipe is outstanding for all saltwater and freshwater fish in the 4- to 10-pound size.
- To prevent lumping, combine roux and dry mustard thoroughly before adding them to liquid.

ANGLING TIP

Use large spoons or minnow-type lures along the edges of weed beds to catch pike.

Steamed Spinach, Pine Nuts and Fish Cheeks

Steamed Spinach, Pine Nuts and Fish Cheeks

1 c. parsnips, cut into 1/8-inch rounds
1/2 c. red onion, sliced 1/4 inch thick
4 c. fresh spinach, stems removed
2 c. fish cheeks, skin on
1/2 c. wild mushrooms, sliced 1/4 inch thick
1/3 c. pine nuts
1/2 c. apple juice
1/2 c. chicken stock (see recipe p. 47) or clam broth
1 tsp. Worcestershire sauce
1/2 tsp. salt
1/8 tsp. black pepper
4 c. cooked grits or white rice

Preheat oven to 375°. Place parsnips and sliced onions in a shallow pan. Top with 2/3 of the spinach. Lay fish cheeks skin side down evenly over spinach. Cover with wild mushrooms and pine nuts. Combine apple juice, chicken broth, Worcestershire sauce, salt and pepper. Add to pan. Top with remaining spinach leaves. Cover with aluminum foil and poke 8 pencil-sized holes in the top.

Bake in a 375° oven for 30 minutes.

Remove from oven. If the spinach leaves are wilted, the dish is done. Serve with grits or white rice.

Serves 4.

CHEF'S TIPS

• If fish cheeks are not available, cut skin-on fish fillets into 1-inch cubes.

• This recipe works very well with 4- to 6-oz. fish steaks.

• For a variation, add 1 cup fresh mushroom slices with fish fillets.

ANGLING TIP

During and right after a good rain is the best time to dip for smelt.

Fish, Leeks and Saffron Velouté

2 T. butter	1 T. cilantro, chopped medium
2 c. leeks, white end sliced 1/4 inch thick	1/4 c. dry white wine
	4 parsley sprigs
2 T. flour	10 saffron threads, minced
1 tsp. salt	1 c. heavy cream
1/8 tsp. white pepper	16 panfish fillets, skin on, scaled
1 pt. fish stock (see recipe p. 47)	1 T. flour for dusting

Heat butter in a Dutch oven. Add leeks and sauté until clear and tender. Sprinkle flour, salt and white pepper over leeks and gently mix to combine. Add fish stock, cilantro, white wine, parsley and saffron. Simmer for 5 minutes. Remove 1/2 cup hot stock and add to cream to temper liquid and prevent curdling. Return cream/stock mixture to liquid slowly. Mix until smooth.

Dust fish fillets with flour. Add fish fillets to broth. Cover and simmer for 1 1/2 to 2 minutes. Remove from heat. Let steep for 5 minutes.

To serve, place 2 cups leeks and broth in a warm soup platter. Top with 4 fish fillets.

Serves 4.

Deep-Fried Smelt

3 to 4 lbs. cleaned smelt	1 tsp. onion or garlic salt
1 qt. milk	1/2 tsp. white pepper
2 c. seasoned flour (see recipe p. 181)	1 tsp. poultry seasoning
	1 qt. vegetable oil
1/2 c. dry cream of wheat	

Soak smelt in milk for 1 hour. In a medium, shallow baking pan or cake pan, combine seasoned flour, cream of wheat, onion or garlic salt, white pepper and poultry seasoning. In an electric frying pan or deep fryer, heat vegetable oil to 375°. Lift smelt from milk to a strainer. Roll no more than 12 to 14 smelt in flour mixture at once to keep smelt flour from forming lumps. When well coated, shake off excess and deep-fry smelt until golden brown. Remove to a paper-towel-lined bowl. Season with your favorite seasoning.

Serves 4 to 6.

- *The cream of wheat creates a crisp crust. For an extra-crispy crust, place the smelt on a rack to dry after rolling it in the flour mixture. When flour is dry, re-dip the smelt in milk and flour mixture. Then fry.*
- *To prevent the frying oil from burning, frequently skim out the crumbs with a fine sieve.*

NOTES

THE RIGHT CHOICE

Opening day of fishing was only two weeks away when the call came. My friend and his son invited my son, Carlton, and me to go to his cabin for a boy's fishing weekend. Carlton was right next to me and lit up like a candle. I asked if we could bring my daughter Brandi along and was told that she was welcome any other time but this was going to be a boy's weekend.

My heart sank. I couldn't imagine leaving Brandi home.

We took a vote and it was unanimous. We knew we had made the right choice.

The Schumacher clan would have it's own fishing outing. We would use our newly purchased "used" boat and shop the catalogues for gear. The night before fishing opener, we spooled line on our new reels, filled our new tackle boxes, traded lures and boasted about who would catch the biggest fish.

The next day we piled into the Suburban and headed to the shallow lake. I backed up the trailer like a pro and unloaded the boat on shore since there was no dock. As I approached the boat, a big gray seagull flew overhead and deposited a large offering on the shoulder of my windbreaker. The kids were sitting stone-faced in the boat. Without a smile or giggle, they said, "That's too bad, Dad," their life jackets shaking from suppressed laughter.

The wind was coming straight at us as I took off my socks and shoes and waded into the water to push the boat on to the lake. As the waves came, I found myself waist deep in the cold water. I plunged into the boat and pulled the starter rope. Nothing. I tried again. Nothing. As the wind blew us towards the shoreline, I realized that I had not connected the gas line.

After connecting the line I pumped the primer ball and pulled the starter rope. The motor revved. I slammed it into reverse and, with a jolt, we shot backwards from shore going full throttle in deep waves. Now if I could only figure out how to go forward.

As I desperately turned the boat to head back to shore, a big green gray wave hit us broadside and we watched our brand new rods and reels glide in slow motion over the side of the boat and into the lake.

We looked down and saw the water that rising in the bottom of the boat. As we drew nearer to shore I jumped into the water and pulled the boat back onto land.

As I cranked the boat back on the trailer Brandi said, "Dad, Dad, the boat has sprung a leak!" Indeed, the boat had a stream of water coming from the drain hole. As I slipped the forgotten drain plug into my coat pocket, I told them that we would let the water run out and fix the leak tomorrow.

To this day Carlton points to the back of all fishing boats and with a sly smile asks, "Hey Dad, do you think those boats leak too?"

Sautéed &
Pan-Fried

Panfish with Sun-Dried Pearl Barley Pilaf

16 boneless panfish fillets, skins on
$\frac{1}{2}$ c. milk
1 c. whole wheat flour
$\frac{1}{4}$ c. vegetable oil
1 T. butter
4 c. sun-dried pearl barley pilaf (see recipe p. 221)

Place fish fillets in a bowl. Add milk. Shake off excess milk and coat with whole wheat flour. Heat vegetable oil in a skillet. When oil is hot, add butter. The butter will bubble. Add fish fillets and fry until golden brown and crisp on both sides. When done, serve with sun-dried pearl barley pilaf and lemon wedges.

Serves 4.

ANGLING TIP

Looking for crappies? Crappies have been known to do well in lakes with large carp populations. Carp create the open water that crappies prefer by thinning dense plant growth.

Fish Beurre Noisette

1/3 c. butter
4 6- to 8-oz. fish fillets
1 c. seasoned flour (see recipe p. 181)
1 T. lemon juice
fresh lemon slices
fresh parsley

In a heavy frying pan, heat butter until light brown in color. Dredge fish in seasoned flour and shake off excess flour. Place in butter, skin side down. Lightly brown. Turn and lightly brown other side. Add lemon juice. Turn off heat. When fillets are flaky when touched with a fork, place them on a heated plate. Top with lemon brown butter from pan. Garnish with lemon slice and parsley.

Serves 4.

CHEF'S TIPS

• *Beurre Noisette* means brown butter in French. To make, heat butter to dark brown before adding fish.

Fried Fish with Caraway Seeds

8 4- to 6-oz. fish fillets
1/2 c. flour
1/4 c. dry cream of wheat
1 tsp. salt
1/8 tsp. white pepper
2 eggs, beaten
1/4 c. milk
1/4 c. lard
1 tsp. caraway seeds
8 dumplings (see recipe p. 218)
1 qt. sweet kraut
4 lemon wedges

Clean fillets and skin fish. Combine flour, cream of wheat, salt and pepper and place in a pie plate. Beat eggs in a bowl with a fork to combine yolks and whites. Add milk and combine. Dredge fillets in flour mixture. Shake off excess. Dip in egg mixture then back in flour.

Heat a large skillet with lard until hot. When lard starts to bubble, add fish fillets flat side down. Fry golden brown. Turn and sprinkle caraway seeds on top of fillets. Fry until golden brown in oil. Remove and place on a hot plate. Serve with dumplings, sweet kraut and lemon wedges.

Serves 4.

CHEF'S TIPS

• If lard is not to your liking, use vegetable oil.
• For a different presentation, fry boiled potato slices in fish oil. Serve the fish with fried potatoes and cream-style corn.

**Oriental Fish Steaks
with Fried Rice**

Oriental Fish Steaks with Fried Rice

1/4 c. soy sauce
1 tsp. brown sugar
2 cloves garlic
1 tsp. fresh ginger
1/2 c. orange juice
2 tsp. cornstarch
pinch ground cinnamon
4 8- to 10-oz. fish steaks
2 T. peanut oil
4 c. fried rice (see recipe p. 210)

Place all sauce ingredients in a blender and puree. Place fish steaks and sauce in a sealable plastic bag and refrigerate for 30 minutes.

To sear fish, heat peanut oil smoke-hot in a skillet. Remove fish fillets from sauce. Shake off excess liquid. Fry until light brown on both sides. Place fillets on a plate. Keep warm in a 200° oven. Shake sauce ingredients in bag to combine well. Add sauce to skillet. Bring to a simmer. Stir with a wooden spoon to keep from scorching. When sauce is thick and clear, remove from heat.

Serve fish over fried rice with sauce.

Serves 4.

CHEF'S TIPS

• By placing steaks in soy sauce mix you are adding flavor to the fish. Soy sauce is very salty, so do not oversoak.

CHEF'S TIPS

• For a variation use fried onion rings or fried sweet potatoes.

• If fresh lime juice is not available, use fresh-squeezed lemon juice.

Barbequed Panfish with Bronzed French Fries

1/4 c. vegetable oil
8 boneless fish fillets
1/2 c. seasoned flour (see recipe p. 181)
2 cloves garlic, diced into 1/4-inch cubes
1/4 c. celery, diced into 1/4-inch cubes
1/4 c. onion, diced into 1/4-inch cubes

1/2 c. red peppers, diced into 1/4-inch cubes
2 tsp. flour
1/2 c. barbeque sauce
2 drops Tabasco sauce
2 tsp. fresh lime juice
1/4 c. dry red wine
1 c. diced tomatoes
4 big handfuls of french fries

Heat oil in a skillet until hot. Toss fish fillets in seasoned flour. Fry fish fillets golden brown on both sides. Place on a platter and keep warm in a 200° oven. Add garlic, celery and onion to fish-flavored oil, and sauté until onions are clear and tender. Add red peppers. To pick up oil, sprinkle flour over top and mix with a wooden spoon. Add barbeque sauce, Tabasco sauce, lime juice and red wine and bring to a boil. Let simmer for 2 minutes on low heat. Add tomatoes. Cover and remove from heat.

Fry french fries until light brown. On large warm plates, place a mound of french fries. Top with fried fish fillets and a generous amount of vegetable sauce.

Serves 4.

CHEF'S TIPS

•Kosher salt has larger, crunchier granules than table salt.

Easy Panfish Chips

20 panfish fillets
1 T. vegetable oil
1 1/2 c. seasoned flour (see recipe p. 181)
2 T. clarified butter (see recipe p. 189)
1 lemon, cut into wedges
kosher salt to taste

Scale and fillet fish. Leave the skin on. In a large skillet, heat the oil until hot. Roll fish fillets in seasoned flour and shake off the excess. Add butter to oil. Place fish in oil, skin side down. Fry for 1 1/2 to 2 minutes. Turn gently and fry again until golden brown. Fish will appear milky white and flake when done. Remove from pan and place on absorbent paper towels. Serve with lemon and kosher salt.

Serves 4.

Frog Legs Provençal

12 pair large frog legs
1½ c. milk
½ c. seasoned flour (see recipe p. 181)
¼ c. clarified butter (see recipe p. 189)
2 cloves garlic, diced into ¼-inch cubes
1 c. tomatoes, diced into ¼-inch cubes
¼ c. black olives, sliced ¼ inch thick
2 tsp. lemon juice
½ c. dry red wine
1 tsp. salt
¼ tsp. black pepper
1 T. fresh thyme

Remove skin from frog legs. Soak in milk for 1 hour. Remove and dredge in seasoned flour. Shake off excess flour. Heat a sauté pan with butter. When butter is bubbling, add garlic and frog legs. Lightly brown legs on one side. Turn legs and add tomatoes, black olives, lemon juice, red wine, salt and pepper. Simmer for 8 minutes on low heat.

Remove to a warm platter. Sprinkle fresh thyme leaves over the top for garnish and serve.

Serves 4.

CHEF'S TIPS

•The larger the frog legs, the better.

ANGLING TIP

Prime time for catfishing is just before and after sunset.

CHEF'S TIPS

- Put each color coulis in a separate squeeze bottle to paint the plates.
- Serve coulis warm on the side with fish.

Pan-Fried Fish with Golden Raisins and Three Colors of Pepper Coulis

1/2 c. seasoned flour (see recipe p. 181)
1 T. chili powder
2 T. olive oil
4 8- to 10-oz. panfish fillets
1/2 c. golden raisins
three colors of pepper coulis (see recipe p. 196)

Combine seasoned flour and chili powder in a pie plate. Heat oil in a skillet. Roll fillets in seasoned flour and shake off the excess. Fry fillets golden brown. Turn fillets. Add raisins and fry other side golden brown. Remove to a warm platter and serve with three colors of pepper coulis.

Serves 4.

CHEF'S TIPS

- This is a classic sauce.
- For a richer variation, add 2 tablespoons of heavy cream when adding the capers.
- If Marsala wine is not available, substitute cream sherry.
- It is important to add the butter last. It adds richness to the sauce.

Fish Piccata

1/4 c. flour
1/2 tsp. salt
1/4 tsp. paprika
1/8 tsp. white pepper
1 1/2 T. light-colored olive oil
4 6- to 8-oz. fish fillets, skins on
2 T. shallots, diced into 1/4-inch pieces

2 tsp. flour
1 T. fresh lemon juice
1 c. dry white wine
1/4 c. Marsala wine
1 T. drained capers
1 T. butter

Combine 1/4 cup flour, salt, paprika and white pepper together and place in a pie pan. In a large skillet, heat oil until hot. Lightly coat fish fillets with flour mixture. Shake off excess. Lay fish fillets skin side down in hot oil. Sauté until skins start to turn golden brown. Gently turn. Sauté about 1 1/2 to 2 minutes. Place on a warm platter. Cover with aluminum foil to keep hot.

Add shallots to the skillet. Stir with wooden spoon. When shallots become transparent, add 2 teaspoons flour, lemon juice, white wine and Marsala wine. Whisk smooth and bring to a rolling boil. Add capers and boil for 3 minutes. Remove from heat. Stir in butter. Spoon sauce over fillets. Garnish with sprigs of fresh tarragon.

Serves 4.

**Pan-Fried Fish with Golden Raisins
and Three Colors of Pepper Coulis**

CHEF'S TIPS

- This is my favorite recipe for bluefish, but other firm, white fillets also work well.

- Leaving the skin on the fillets helps keep the fish pieces intact.

- The vegetables look and cook best if sliced Chinese-style or on the bias.

Fish Stir-Fry

1 c. onion sliced ¼ inch thick
1 c. carrots, sliced ¼ inch thick on the bias
1 c. celery, sliced ¼ inch thick on the bias
1 c. red pepper, sliced ¼ inch thick, 3 inches long
1 c. fresh mushrooms, sliced ¼ inch thick
1½ T. vegetable oil or saffron oil
1 T. cornstarch
1 T. soy sauce
1 tsp. fresh gingerroot, minced fine
2 c. chicken stock, fish stock (see recipe p. 47) or clam broth
3 c. fish fillets, sliced into finger-sized pieces, skin on
4 c. cooked white rice (see recipe p. 211)

Peel and cut vegetables. In a wok or heavy sauté pan, heat oil until smoke-hot. Add vegetables and cook for 3 minutes, turning gently to keep them from burning. Combine cornstarch, soy sauce, fresh ginger and chicken stock. Add to vegetables and bring to a simmer. Add fish, tossing gently, and cook until fish is tender and sauce is clear. Remove and serve over white rice.

Serves 4.

CHEF'S TIPS

- My mother always made panfish this way on the farm. She served them with her hash browns (see recipe p. 203). It is my favorite recipe for panfish.

- Have a dish handy for fish bones. Advise your guests that taking the time to remove bones before eating is well worth the extra time and effort.

Fried Whole Panfish

12 whole panfish
1½ c. vegetable oil
¼ c. butter
1½ c. seasoned flour (see recipe p. 181)
lemon for squeezing

Scale and remove head and insides from fish. Remove the dorsal fin and leave the tail on. Wash fish well in cold water.

In deep pan, heat vegetable oil to 375°. Add butter. Roll fish in seasoned flour and shake off excess. Place fish in pan and brown to a golden color. Turn and brown on the other side. When fish are done, remove to a plate lined with absorbent paper towels. Serve with fresh lemon.

Serves 4.

Mushroom Sand-Bronzed Fish Triangles

8 4-oz. fish fillets, skins on
$^{1}/_{2}$ c. milk
$^{1}/_{2}$ c. mushroom flour meal (see mushroom flour meal and variations recipe p. 180)
1 T. olive oil
$^{1}/_{2}$ c. chicken stock (see recipe p. 47)
1 T. anchovy, mashed to a paste
$^{1}/_{4}$ c. heavy cream
1 c. fresh mushrooms, sliced thin
1 tsp. dry tarragon
$^{1}/_{8}$ tsp. white pepper

Place fish fillets in a bowl with milk. Remove and shake off excess milk. Dredge fish fillets in mushroom flour. Press to coat well and shake off excess.

Heat olive oil in a skillet. When hot, add fish fillets and cook until brown. Turn and repeat. Remove to a warm paper-towel-lined plate until service.

Add chicken stock and anchovy paste to pan and bring to a boil. Boil for 2 minutes, reducing liquid. Reduce heat to a simmer. Slowly drizzle in cream. Stir until smooth. Add mushroom slices, tarragon leaves and white pepper. Let simmer for 2 minutes.

To serve, place 2 fish fillets on a warm dinner plate. Top with sauce and mushroom slices.

Serves 4.

CHEF'S TIPS

- The recipe got its name because mushroom flour meal has the consistency of sand.
- Making mushroom flour meal is time consuming. If you do not have the time to make it, use coarse-ground whole wheat flour.

ANGLING TIP

In the springtime, walleyes are very aggressive and will hit just about any lure.

Fish Casino

Fish Casino

2 T. butter
4 8- to 10-oz. fish fillets
½ c. seasoned flour (see recipe p. 181)
1 T. olive oil
½ c. red pepper, diced into ¼-inch pieces
½ c. green pepper, diced into ¼-inch pieces
½ c. green onion, sliced ¼ inch thick
1 T. capers, drained
½ c. cooked bacon, diced into ¼-inch pieces
1 tsp. Worcestershire sauce
1 whole lemon, cut into 4 wedges

In a large frying pan, heat butter to a fast bubble. Dredge fish in seasoned flour and shake off excess flour. Place fish in butter and fry until golden brown. Gently turn fish and reduce heat and cook for 2 to 3 minutes or until tender.

While fish are cooking, heat olive oil in a medium frying pan. Add peppers and green onions. Sauté for 1 minute. Add capers, cooked bacon and Worcestershire sauce. Combine gently. Remove cooked fish fillets and place on a warm serving platter. Top fish fillets with casino mixture and serve with lemon wedges.

Serves 4.

CHEF'S TIPS

• This is an outstanding recipe for all fish fillets and steaks.

CHEF'S TIPS

• To rice potatoes, place cooked potatoes in ricer bin and squeeze the hand grips. The extended potato pieces will look like rice.

• Potato ricers can be difficult to find. Check with specialty kitchen stores to find one for your kitchen.

Fish Florence

4 white baking potatoes
¼ c. clarified butter (see recipe p. 189)
½ c. shallots or red onion, diced into ¼-inch pieces
3 c. fish pieces, cut into 1-inch squares
¼ c. seasoned flour (see recipe p. 181)
¼ tsp. dry mustard
1 tsp. paprika
¼ tsp. salt
pinch white pepper
¼ c. dry sherry wine
1 c. heavy cream
1½ c. fresh mushrooms, cut into quarters

Peel white baking potatoes. Cut in half and boil to just tender in salted water. Drain off all water and let potatoes steam off for 2 minutes. Cover with a cotton towel. Keep warm for service.

In a heavy sauté pan, melt butter. Add shallots and cook until transparent. Add fish and sauté until fish sets and the color is milk-white. Turn fish. Combine flour, dry mustard, paprika, salt and pepper. Sprinkle over fish. Toss very gently to combine. Add sherry, cream and mushrooms. Bring to a boil and simmer on low heat 4 to 5 minutes.

To serve, rice potatoes in the center of a warm plate. Top with fish and sauce.

Serves 4.

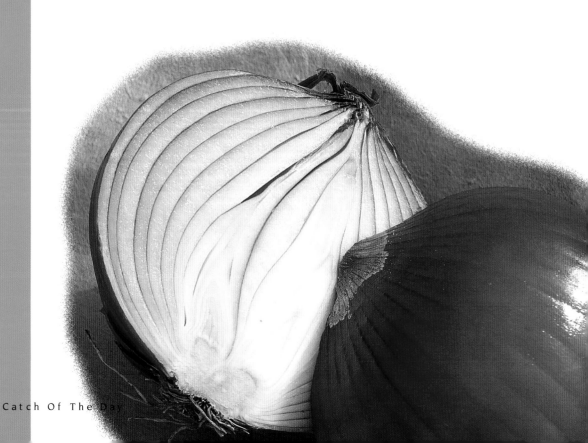

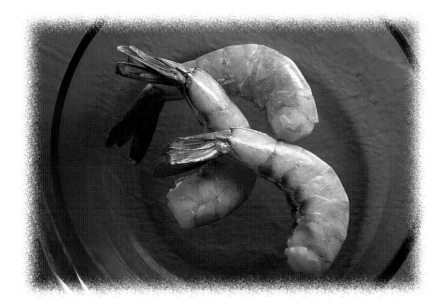

CHEF'S TIPS

- This is best with sweeter types of fish such as walleye, pike, redfish, Dover sole, trout and Arctic char.
- Buttered egg noodles or spätzle is a great side dish with this recipe.

Fish, Shrimp and Scallop Fricassee

1/4 c. butter
1/2 c. shallots, sliced 1/4 inch thick
2 cloves garlic, minced fine
1 c. celery, cut into match-sized strips
1 c. parsnips, cut into match-sized strips
1 c. carrots, cut into match-sized strips
1 1/2 c. fish or chicken stock (see recipe p. 47)
12 raw shrimp, shells on
1 c. dry red wine
1/3 c. tomato puree
1/4 c. heavy cream
2 tsp. fresh tarragon
2 c. sea scallops
8 fish fillets, cut into 2-inch pieces
1/3 c. seasoned flour (see recipe p. 181)
1 tsp. chopped chives

Heat butter to a bubble in a large skillet. Add shallots, garlic, celery, parsnips and carrots. Stir gently with a wooden spoon until carrots are just tender. Add stock and shrimp and sauté 1 minute. Add red wine, tomato puree, heavy cream and tarragon and bring to a rolling boil. Roll scallops and fish pieces in seasoned flour. Add chives, scallops and fish to skillet. Simmer for 5 minutes.

On large, warmed dinner plates, spoon 2 fish fillets onto the center of each plate. Add scallops. Place shrimp around the edge of the plate. Spoon vegetables on the top of fish.

Serves 4.

CHEF'S TIPS

- I prefer using lake trout for this recipe.
- Serve with 3 small dollops of Wasabi on the side of each plate. Wasabi is green Japanese horseradish.

Fish Fillets with Honey Mustard Sauce

4 4- to 6-oz. fish fillets
1 c. seasoned flour (see recipe p. 181)
1 T. butter
1 tsp. lemon juice
1/3 c. honey mustard sauce (see recipe p. 177)
4 sprigs fresh tarragon
4 lemon wedges

Cut fish fillets in 4-inch-wide pieces, leaving the skin on. Roll in seasoned flour and sauté in butter on both sides to golden brown (about 5 to 6 minutes). Splash with lemon juice.

To serve, spoon honey mustard sauce in center of plate. Top with fish fillets and garnish with tarragon and lemon wedges.

Serves 4.

Farmwife Fish Fillets

1 c. flour
1 tsp. dry mustard
1 tsp. salt
1/2 tsp. white pepper
2 T. butter
4 to 6 medium skinless fish fillets
1/2 c. fresh lemon juice
1 tsp. fresh dill weed, minced
2 tsp. dill pickles, diced into 1/4-inch cubes
8 slices fresh bread

Preheat oven to 350°.

Combine flour, dry mustard, salt and white pepper. Sift out any lumps.

In a heavy pan, heat butter to a fast bubble. Coat fillets in flour mix and shake off excess flour. Add to pan and brown. Turn and bake in a 350° oven 5 minutes or until fillets are tender. They should be flaky and milky white. Place fish fillets on a warm serving plate. Add lemon juice, dill weed and dill pickles to butter mixture. Bring to a boil. Place fillets on top of 2 slices fresh bread and top with dill/butter sauce.

Serves 4.

CHEF'S TIPS

- If you do not have dill pickles, use capers.
- Finish the fish in the oven to keep them tender and moist.
- Sourdough bread or homemade bread is the best.

ANGLING TIP

When fishing for salmon moving upstream in the fall, use spawn sacs, yarn flies and streamer flies.

Walleye and Morel Mushrooms

4 8- to 10-oz. walleye fillets, skins on
12 small to medium morel mushrooms
¼ c. clarified butter (see recipe p. 189)
1 c. seasoned flour (see recipe p. 181)
1 T. lemon juice
1 c. dry white wine
2 tsp. fresh tarragon, minced fine

Fillet walleye. Wash and drain morel mushrooms and pat dry on a paper towel. In a large frying pan, heat butter to a fast bubble. Dredge fish in seasoned flour and shake off excess flour. Place fish in clarified butter. Cook walleye fillets until golden brown. Turn fillets and add mushrooms. Splash with lemon juice. Turn mushrooms. Add white wine and tarragon.

Serves 4.

Quick and Easy Crunchy Fish

4 6- to 8-oz. boneless fish fillets
1 c. Parmesan cheese, shredded
1 c. cornmeal
1 tsp. fresh dill weed, diced fine
1 c. vegetable oil
¼ c. butter
1 c. seasoned flour (see recipe p. 181)
1 c. egg wash (see recipe p. 181)
1 tsp. fresh lemon juice
seasoning of choice
1 lemon, cut into wedges

Skin and fillet fish. Cut slabs into 4 pieces. If fillets are thick, slice on the bias.

Mix Parmesan cheese, cornmeal and dill weed in a pie pan. Heat oil in an electric fry pan to 375°. When oil is hot, add butter.

Dredge fish in seasoned flour. Shake off excess flour. Dip fish in egg wash and roll in cornmeal mixture. Shake off excess cornmeal and place in hot oil. Brown on one side for about 2 minutes. Turn fish and cook until done. Remove from oil and place on absorbent paper towels. Lightly splash with lemon juice.

Serves 4.

CHEF'S TIPS

• Walleye and morel mushrooms are among the great treasures of the Heartland. Both need tender, loving care to prepare correctly.

CHEF'S TIPS

• Dust fish with your favorite seasoning such as Cajun, lemon pepper or garlic salt.

• Use your favorite sauce or salsa as a dipping sauce.

Fish Beurre Blanc

4 8-oz. skinless fish fillets
1 c. seasoned flour
(see recipe p. 181)
1 T. clarified butter
(see recipe p. 189)

2 T. chopped shallots
1½ c. dry white wine
¼ tsp. salt
ground white pepper to taste
12 lemon medallions

Preheat oven to 350°.

Dredge fillets in seasoned flour. In a large frying pan, heat clarified butter to a fast bubble. Add shallots and fish fillets. Sauté for 1 minute. Turn fish fillets over. Add wine and cover.

Bake in a 350° oven for 15 minutes. Remove fillets. Add salt and white pepper to finish sauce. Return to heat and simmer for 15 seconds. Remove fillets to a warm dinner plate. Pour two tablespoons of sauce over each fillet. Garnish each fillet with three lemon medallions and a fresh flower for color.

Serves 4.

Sautéed Fillets with Peach and Black Cherry Chutney

4 8- to 10-oz. boneless fish fillets
½ c. seasoned flour (see recipe p. 181)
¼ tsp. black pepper
2 T. peanut oil
1 c. peach and black cherry chutney (see recipe p. 196)
4 c. long-grain white rice, steamed (see recipe p. 211)

Dredge moist fillets in seasoned flour. Let sit on a rack for 5 minutes. Add black pepper to peanut oil. Heat peanut oil to medium-hot. Add fillets and fry until golden brown on both sides. Remove to a paper-towel-lined pan to let oil drain off. To serve, place on a warm serving plate accompanied by peach and black cherry chutney and steamed long-grain white rice.

Serves 4.

CHEF'S TIPS

• Recommended fish for this dish include walleye, pike, trout, cod, scrod, lemon sole, orange roughy and red snapper.

CHEF'S TIPS

• With the addition of mild peppers, the fruit and berry combination is enhanced.

•I first enjoyed this
dish in Sydney, Aus-
tralia at the Bather's
Pavilion Restaurant.

•This recipe is not
as difficult as it looks
and is well worth
the effort.

Seared Fish with Garlic Sour Cream Potatoes and Crisp Onion Shreds

4 red potatoes, peeled and cut in half
1/2 tsp. salt
4 cloves garlic, cut in half
1 1/2 c. celery, peeled and cut into 1-inch pieces
1 c. sour cream
1/2 tsp. salt
1/8 tsp. white pepper
1/4 c. peanut oil
4 6- to 8-oz. fish steaks
2 onions, sliced paper thin
2 T. cornstarch
1 lemon, cut into 4 wedges

Wash and peel potatoes. Boil in 1 quart salted water with garlic and celery. When potatoes are tender, drain water. Let steam, uncovered, for 2 minutes. Add sour cream, salt and white pepper, then mash. Cover and hold for service.

In a skillet, heat oil almost smoke-hot. Add fish steaks. Fry until golden brown and turn. Fry other side golden brown. Place fish on a hot plate. Cover with a cotton towel. Let oil return to hot. Toss onions with cornstarch and shake off excess. Sprinkle onions into hot oil. Fry until crisp. Remove with a skimmer to paper-towel-lined plate.

To assemble, set out 4 warm dinner plates. Place a generous amount of potatoes in the center of each plate. Lean a fish steak on one side of the mound of potatoes. Top with onion shreds. Serve with a generous wedge of lemon.

Serves 4.

NOTES

THE HOUSE OF HARDY

My daughter Brandi spent a semester of college in England. When my wife and I visited, she told us about a great fishing shop in the nearby village of Alnwick. That afternoon, we drove to the House of Hardy store.

Two English gentlemen greeted us. I told them that we were visiting from Minnesota, USA. They just looked at each other and nodded. My wife Kathleen quietly whispered, "Maybe we are in the wrong place with our blue jeans."

Not to be deterred, I asked them about the store and the crown logos. "Sir," said one of them in a clipped British accent, "We are the House of Hardy and those logos are the royal seal of the Queen. We make fishing equipment for the royal family." I asked, "Do you have any spinning rods?" Another blunder. "Sir, we make the finest fly fishing equipment in the world but we may have one or two rods for pike fishing in Ireland. Please come this way," the other man said.

They ushered us to a room with handmade fly rods on a custom display. I saw the most impressive spinning rods I'd ever seen. I also noticed photos of well-heeled fisherman standing in streams, gently holding salmon. A card with prices was attached to each photo. I asked, "You rent rods, too?"

A look of shock crossed their faces. "Sir, we do not rent rods. Those prices are for salmon fishing leases, which include the fly fishing rods." As I looked again, I saw that for one person to fish for a week cost 8000 pounds and the best one could hope for was catching about one fish per day.

I blurted out, "Let me tell you about salmon fishing in Alaska. I've caught up to twenty king salmon weighing up to 48 pounds in one day!" They asked, "How did you manage that?" and I replied, " I simply used a pink spoon with a small piece of salmon spawn."

They could not conceal their contempt. "Sir, we would never allow that. It's not cricket." My wife and daughter held their breath waiting to see what I would do next. With a wave of my hand, I picked out a spinning rod and instructed the salesman to add one of the fancy leather rod cases, a box of hand made Hardy flies and an expensive Hardy corduroy vest, and then pulled out my credit card. We bade them farewell. When I arrived back home, the credit card charges had been converted from pounds into dollars and it definitely wasn't cricket!

I still have my beautiful House of Hardy rod with its silk bag, leather travel case and royal seal. I have yet to use it, but it makes me smile every time I think of those two salesmen and their reaction to the brash, Midwestern American who knew nothing about their famous company.

Note: Since 1872, the House of Hardy has been known as one of the world's finest fishing tackle companies.

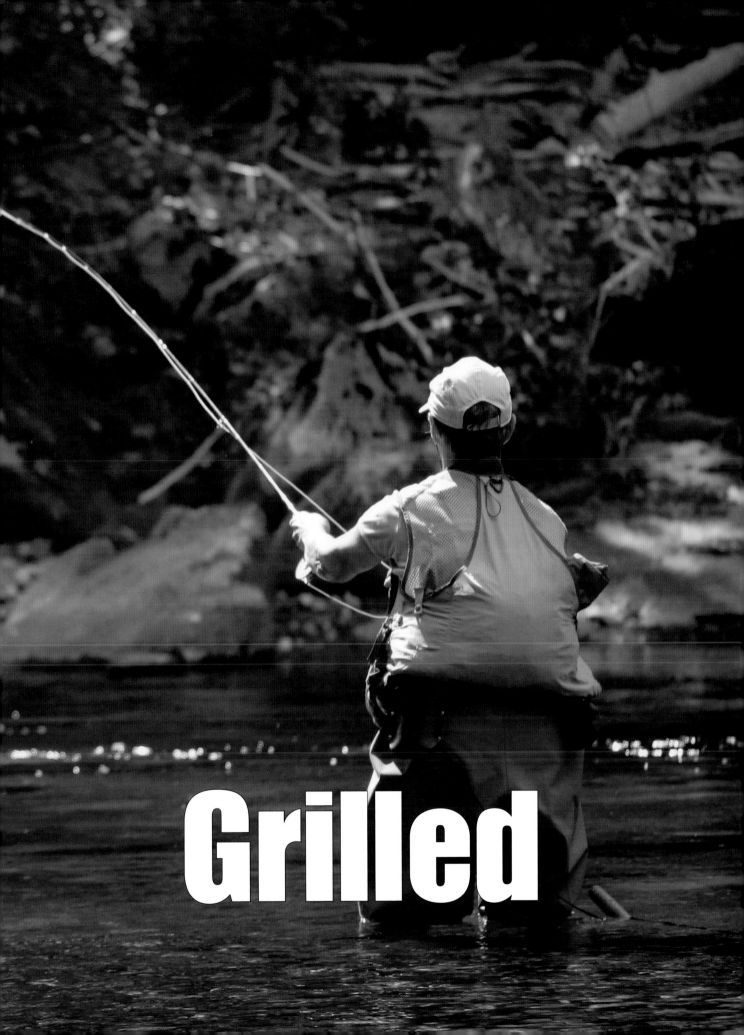

Grilled

Grilled Five-Spice Fish Steaks

Sauce

1 tsp. fresh gingerroot, peeled, diced fine
2 T. peanut oil
1/4 c. dry white wine
2 T. soy sauce
1 T. five-spice powder (see recipe p. 184)
1/4 c. barbeque demi-glace (see recipe p. 172)
1 tsp. fresh lime juice

• • • • •

4 8- to 10-oz. fish steaks, skins on

peanut oil for grilling

Combine all sauce ingredients. Blend until smooth. Place in a large sealable plastic bag with fish steaks. Turn over a few times to coat steaks. Let flavors fuse for at least 1 hour in refrigerator.

Heat grill medium-hot. Brush grates with peanut oil. Remove steaks from bag and brush lightly with marinade. Place on grill for 3 minutes. Turn over. Baste each with 1 teaspoon marinade and grill 3 minutes. Serve with fried or white rice.

Serves 4.

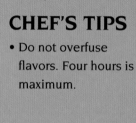

CHEF'S TIPS

• Do not overfuse flavors. Four hours is maximum.

ANGLING TIP

When choosing lures, remember that fish use hearing, smell and sight to locate food. For predator fish, hearing is most important.

Pineapple-Lime-Honey Grilled Fish

¼ c. honey
¼ c. pineapple juice
1 T. fresh lime juice
1 tsp. gingerroot minced fine
¼ c. red onion, cut into ¼-inch pieces
1 T. soy sauce
4 6- to 8-oz. fish steaks or fillets
1 large ripe pineapple

Combine honey, pineapple juice, lime juice, ginger, red onion and soy sauce in a shallow bowl. Place fish in bowl. Cover and refrigerate for 2 to 3 hours. Cut whole pineapple into quarter wedges. Keep the leaves on. With a grapefruit knife, loosen pineapple from rind. Leave about 1 inch in the center to keep intact with the rind. Lay wedges on side and cut the hard darker yellow center core out (about 1 inch deep).

Heat grill medium-hot and brush with oil. Place fish steaks on grill. Brush honey liquid generously over pineapple wedges and place them rind side down on grill. Be careful when grilling fish because the honey liquid will burn rather quickly. After 4 minutes, turn fish steaks. Baste top with more honey liquid. Brush pineapple again with liquid and turn pineapple wedges over. Grill fish about 4 to 5 minutes and check for doneness. Remove to a warm platter. Place a wedge of hot pineapple in between fish pieces.

Serves 4.

CHEF'S TIPS

• I also roast green bananas with this recipe. Brush or spray the outside of the banana skin with vegetable oil. Place on the grill and roast dark brown to black on all sides. When both fish and pineapples are ready, serve with a hot skinned banana. To eat, cut off one end of the banana and squeeze out the warm, soft banana sauce. Splash with fresh lime juice.

Grilled Fish Steaks with Fruited Chili Sambal

4 8- to 10-oz. fish steaks, skins on
2 T. peanut oil for grilling
lime juice
1 c. fruited chili sambal (see recipe p. 198)

Heat grill medium-hot. Brush grate and fish steaks with peanut oil. Grill golden brown on each side for about 5 minutes. Splash with lime juice and serve on a bed of steamed rice or boiled sweet potatoes with a ramekin of warm sambal.

Serves 4.

CHEF'S TIPS

• Sambal is a hot sauce. Warn family and friends before serving!

**Grilled Fish and
Eggplant Roma**

Grilled Fish and Eggplant Roma

1/2 c. olive oil
8 2- to 3-oz. fish fillets
4 red onion slices, 1/2 inch thick
4 eggplant slices, 1/2 inch thick
8 tomato slices, 1/2 inch thick
4 red pepper ring slices, 1/2 inch thick
1 qt. spaghetti sauce, heated
salt and black pepper to taste
1 T. fresh cilantro
1 T. fresh basil
3 c. mozzarella cheese, shredded

Heat grill medium-hot. Brush fish and vegetables with olive oil. Place spaghetti sauce in a small pot on the side of the grill. Place onions and eggplant on the grill and grill for 3 minutes. Place fish, tomatoes and peppers on grill. Turn and season with salt and pepper.

To assemble, place fish fillets and pepper rings on eggplant. Put a little spaghetti sauce in each pepper ring. Add a fish fillet and top with red onions. Add more sauce and evenly season with herbs. Add tomato slices, more sauce, and top with cheese. Remove from grill with an oiled, wide spatula to a warm platter.

Serves 4.

CHEF'S TIPS

• Use your imagination with all your favorite vegetables and spices.

Grilled Fish with Curry Ghee

1 c. flour
2 tsp. curry powder (see recipe p. 185)
4 6- to 8-oz. fish fillets, scaled, skin on
1/4 c. sesame oil
1/2 c. curry ghee (see recipe p. 190)
4 lime wedges

Combine flour and curry powder in a shallow baking pan. Dredge fillets in flour mixture and shake off excess. Place fish in a grilling rack and shut tightly. Heat grill medium-hot. Brush oil on grates. Lightly brush sesame oil over both sides of fish. Place on grill skin side down. Cook until golden brown. Turn and repeat. Remove fish to a large serving platter. Serve with white rice and top with curry ghee and wedges of lime.

Serves 4.

CHEF'S TIPS

• Sesame oil has a very strong, dominating flavor. If sesame is not a flavor you enjoy, substitute a milder vegetable oil.

CHEF'S TIPS

SCHUMACHER'S RULES FOR SERVICE:

- No poking family with hot forks.
- Pinching with tongs is legal.
- A few salty words are acceptable.
- Most importantly, season with love and serve with a smile.

- This recipe is fun and challenging. You will need at least two helpers to pull this off.

Grilled Fish and Vegetable Picnic

8 medium carrots, peeled
8 red peppers, cut in half
16 mild chili peppers, stem and seeds removed
16 large asparagus spears
8 plum tomatoes
4 medium zucchini
8 Bartlett pears, cores removed
8 medium red potatoes
2 large eggplants, cut into 1/2-inch- thick slices
1/4 c. salt
1 head cauliflower
8 small yellow onions, peeled
2 pts. herbed salad dressing
8 10-oz. fish steaks, 1 inch thick
2 large loaves of French bread, cut in half lengthwise
tons of butter
salt and pepper to taste

You will need a giant grill or 2 to 3 small grills for the whole feast!

Peel carrots. Remove stem end and seeds from red peppers and mild chili peppers. Trim 1 to 1 1/2 inches off bottom of asparagus spears. Remove stem ends from tomatoes and zucchini. With an apple corer, remove cores from Bartlett pears. Scrub the outside of the potatoes clean. Slice eggplant and brush with lemon juice to keep from darkening. Heat a large pot half full of water and add 1/4 cup salt. Bring water to a rolling boil. Put in whole cauliflower. Cover, and as soon as water returns to a boil, remove cauliflower with a skimmer. Plunge cauliflower into ice-cold water to stop cooking. When cauliflower is well chilled, place upside down on a rack to drain out the water. Cut in half.

By now, water should be back to boiling. Add potatoes, carrots and onions. Boil 15 minutes. Remove from heat. Drain all water and let vegetables steam off for 10 minutes. Remove to pan to be cooled in the refrigerator. Next cut deep X's on both sides of zucchini. Wrap asparagus in double-thick foil with 1/4 cup butter.

In a large pan, put 2 pints herbed salad dressing. Place a wire rack in another pan for draining off dressing.

It takes 30 to 35 minutes to cook the entire meal. The grills should be hot. Roll peppers, zucchini, potatoes and pears in herbed dressing and set on rack to drain briefly. Then place on grill. Keep all vegetables in their own groups. Next place asparagus package on grill. Coat carrots and onions with herbed dressing. Drain and add to grill. Coat eggplant slices, tomatoes and cauliflower halves with herb dressing and drain. Place on grill. By this time you need to start turning the first vegetables. Coat and drain fish and add to grill.

Lastly add hot peppers. Salt and pepper vegetables to taste. On top of everything, add French bread halves that are well buttered. Brush everything in sight with melted butter. Turn fish. Call the troops and start serving.

Serves 8.

CHEF'S TIPS

• Consider serving fish steaks atop horseradish mashed potatoes. The flavors work well together.

Grilled Fish with Mustard-Dill Sour Cream Sauce

4 6- to 8-oz. fish fillets or steaks
¼ c. peanut oil
1 T. lemon juice
1 tsp. Worcestershire sauce
1 c. mustard-dill sour cream sauce (see recipe p. 173)

Heat grill to medium. Brush fish with peanut oil. Place on grill. Lightly splash lemon juice over fish. Grill for 3 minutes. Turn to make crisscross markings. Grill 2 minutes more. Turn steaks with a broad spatula. Splash top with lemon juice and Worcestershire sauce and grill 3 to 4 minutes.

To serve, place fish on a warm plate and pour a ribbon of mustard-dill sour cream sauce over one side.

Serves 4.

ANGLING TIP

When fishing for salmon moving upstream in the fall, use spawn sacs, yarn flies and streamer flies.

Grilled Fish T-Bone Steaks with Anchovy-Caper Butter

CHEF'S TIPS

• Boneless steaks and fillets work just as well as bone-in steaks.

2 T. olive oil
4 10-oz. bone-in fish steaks
2 tsp. Worcestershire sauce
anchovy-caper butter (see recipe p. 190)

Heat grill medium-hot. Brush grill and steaks with olive oil. Place fish steaks on grill. Cook for 3 minutes. Turn to mark with a crisscross pattern and grill for 3 more minutes. Turn steaks over and repeat grilling. When testing for doneness, test meat closest to the bone. When steaks are medium rare, splash with Worcestershire sauce and remove to warm serving platter. Cut a 1-inch slice of anchovy-caper butter and put on top of each steak. Serve with a wedge of lemon.

Serves 4.

Grilled 3-Pepper Fish Steaks with Herbed Cream Sauce

CHEF'S TIPS

• This needs a strong-flavored fish such as salmon, catfish or marlin.

• Do not let fish steaks fuse in the dressing for more than 6 hours.

1 c. herbed dressing
1½ T. 3-pepper blend, coarsely ground
4 8- to 10-oz. fish steaks, skin on
2 c. herbed cream sauce (see recipe p. 175)

Place herbed dressing and coarsely ground pepper blend in a large sealable plastic bag. Shake well to combine. Add fish steaks. Lay flat on a pan. Let flavors fuse for 1 hour in refrigerator. Heat grill medium-hot. Brush grill racks with oil. Place steaks on grill. Make sure a few pieces of pepper blend are on top and sides. Grill 3 minutes. Turn to mark with a crisscross pattern and grill 3 more minutes. Turn steaks over gently with a broad spatula. Add a few pieces of peppercorns. Grill 3 to 4 minutes.

To serve, place ½ cup of herbed cream sauce in the center of a warm plate. Top with a grilled steak.

Serves 4.

Grilled Fish T-Bone Steaks with Anchovy-Caper Butter

CHEF'S TIPS

• Compote can be served warm or cold.

• The addition of 2 tablespoons Grand Marnier to the compote tastes great.

• Rice pilaf or grits make good accompaniments with this dish.

ANGLING TIP

Medium- or medium-heavy-action rods are best for jig-fishing walleyes.

Grilled Fish with Ruby Red Grapefruit and Lemon-Mango Compote

2 T. vegetable oil
½ T. soy sauce
2 tsp. fresh gingerroot, minced fine
4 8- to 10-oz. fish steaks
1 to 2 c. ruby red grapefruit and lemon-mango compote
(see recipe p. 193)

Blend oil, soy sauce and ginger in a blender until smooth. Place in a sealable plastic bag. Add fish steaks and let flavoring fuse for 1 hour.

Heat grill medium-hot. Grill fish, making marks on both sides. It takes about 10 to 12 minutes. Serve on a hot dinner plate with chilled ruby red grapefruit and lemon-mango compote.

Serves 4.

Grilled Fish Steaks

4 fish steaks, 1 inch thick
1 T. lemon juice
1 tsp. lemon zest, grated
1 T. vegetable oil
black pepper
salt to taste

Place fish steaks, lemon juice, lemon zest, 1 tablespoon vegetable oil and black pepper in a sealable plastic bag and let flavor fuse for at least 1 hour. Turn once or twice to have both sides fused.

Preheat the grill to hot. Brush or spray grate with vegetable oil. Grill fish steaks for 2 minutes and turn them to make a crisscross mark. Gently lift steaks with a broad spatula and turn over. Grill for 2 minutes and turn them to make a crisscross mark. Fish steaks should be cooked medium-rare or at very most medium.

Place on a platter. Lightly sprinkle with kosher or your favorite flavored salt.

Serves 4.

- *The thickness of the fish steak is very important. A minimum of 1 to 1 1/2 inches is best for fish steaks (boneless or bone-in). The thickness helps keep the moisture in the meat, as fish have very little to no fat. If the juice is cooked out, you are left with no flavor.*
- *Letting fish sit too long in lemon and oil will make the fish soft and mushy.*

Whole Fish Grilled in Apple Bacon

1 4- to 5-lb. whole fish
1 c. boiled potatoes, sliced in 1/4-inch slices
4 shallots, diced into 1/4-inch cubes
1 c. green apple, unpeeled and shredded
2 sprigs fresh tarragon or thyme
1/2 tsp. lemon zest, grated fine
1 tsp. lemon juice
1/8 tsp. freshly ground black pepper
1 to 1 1/2 lb. apple-smoked bacon, sliced thick

Scale the fish well on both sides, back and belly. Remove insides, gills and eyes. With a vegetable brush, lightly clean fish inside and out. Run cold water over fish inside and out. In cavity, place potato slices, shallots, shredded apple, tarragon or thyme sprigs, lemon zest, lemon juice and pepper. Make sure potatoes are inside fish. Wrap bacon around fish, overlapping to form the crust. Do not wrap head and tail. Wrap tail in a double-thick piece of foil to keep it from burning.

Heat grill medium-hot. Place fish in fish rack. Brush fish lightly with vegetable oil. Set rack on grill. Turn every 4 to 5 minutes until bacon is brown and fish is tender, about 30 minutes. While grilling, make sure there is not a flare-up from dripping bacon fat and fish/vegetable juices. The thickest part, closest to the fish head, takes the longest to cook. When testing for doneness, test meat closest to the bone. When cooked, place fish on a platter. Remove foil from tail. Slice into 2- to 3-inch slabs. When serving, remind guests about bones.

Serves 4.

CHEF'S TIPS

• This method works the same for freshwater and saltwater fish.
• You can purchase a cast-iron smoke box to place over the coals or gas burner. Fill it with wet wood chips to give the fish a smoked flavor.
• Don't sprinkle salt on the fish prior to cooking, as it will draw out moisture and dry out the fish.

CHEF'S TIPS

• For a recipe variation, pour 1/4 cup barbeque sauce over shallots and potatoes inside the fish cavity before wrapping with bacon. To roast in oven, set heat at 400° and bake for 30 to 35 minutes. Test often for doneness!

**Barbequed Fish with
Sweet Potato Medallions**

Grilled Mushroom-Crusted Fish on Mushroom Risotto

4 6- to 8-oz. fillets
1 c. milk
1/2 c. mushroom flour (see recipe p. 180)
1/2 c. instant potato granules
vegetable oil
4 c. mushroom risotto (see recipe p. 207)

Place fish steaks in a shallow bowl with milk. Combine mushroom flour and potato granules in a pie plate. Remove fish steaks from milk. Shake off excess milk. Dredge in mushroom/flour mix. Press to coat well. Shake off excess. Heat grill to medium. Spray steak with vegetable oil. Brush grill with oil and place fish on grill. Cook for 4 minutes. Very gently slip an oiled, wide spatula under steaks. Lift steaks. Spray one more time with vegetable spray and turn back on grill. Cook until brown and medium-rare. Remove from grill and serve with mushroom risotto.

Serves 4.

Barbequed Fish with Sweet Potato Medallions

4 small or 2 large sweet potatoes
1/4 c. brown sugar
1/2 tsp. nutmeg
4 8- to 10-oz. fish steaks
1/2 c. olive oil
1/4 c. butter
1 c. barbeque sauce of choice
4 lemon wedges

Wash and cut sweet potatoes into 1/2-inch-thick rounds. Boil in salted water for 10 minutes. Drain off water and let potatoes steam off. Keep refrigerated until needed. In small bowl, combine brown sugar and nutmeg.

Heat grill medium-hot. Brush fish steaks and sweet potato slices with olive oil. Place fish and sweet potatoes on grill and cook for 3 minutes. Turn to make crisscross marks. Let cook 3 minutes more. Turn over. Brush tops with soft butter. Sprinkle with brown sugar mixture. Top with barbeque sauce. Shut lid and cook 3 to 4 minutes. When fish is medium-rare, place fish steaks and sweet potatoes on a platter. Serve with lemon wedges.

Serves 4.

CHEF'S TIPS

- The mushroom flour takes considerable time to make.
- Be sure to use an oiled, wide spatula for turning and removing fish from grill.
- If the crust starts to brown too fast, move it to the slower side of the grill or turn down the heat and shut the lid. It is important to spray mushroom crust well with vegetable oil to keep it from burning. If you do not have vegetable spray, place 1/4 c. vegetable oil on a plate and coat both sides of the fish in oil before grilling.

CHEF'S TIPS

- If desired, mashed sweet potatoes can be made after removing from grill. Place potatoes in a bowl with 1 tablespoon butter and1 tablespoon cream. Mash and serve under steaks.

Tea-Smoking Base Recipe

1 c. strong-brewed tea
¼ c. brown sugar
1 T. white sugar
1 c. uncooked long-grained white rice

Combine tea, sugars and rice in a glass jar. Cover and refrigerate until ready to use.

After heating the tea/rice base so that it has smoked for 3 minutes, add bread slices with food item atop. Smoke for 3 minutes. Set aside, covered, for 20 minutes. Remove smoked food from pan. Use as desired. Discard bread and tea base.

Tea-Smoking Process

I was introduced to this traditional Chinese method of smoking seafood, meats, fish and vegetables in several of the outstanding restaurants in Sydney, Australia.

It is a unique, easy way to smoke food. Tea-smoking imparts a very rich, smoky flavor. Select a wok or Dutch oven that will be used only for smoking purposes. Make sure that the rack that will be placed in the smoking pan is at least 3 or more inches off the bottom of the pan. This will prevent food from being overcooked on the bottom.

The pan will be filled as follows:

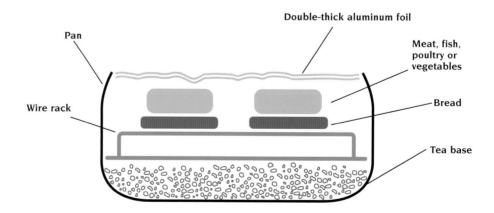

Double-thick aluminum foil

Pan

Meat, fish, poultry or vegetables

Wire rack

Bread

Tea base

CHEF'S TIPS

• I recommend jasmine or orange pekoe teas.

CHEF'S TIPS

• Bread slices will keep the food from sticking to the rack and prevent overcooking the bottom of the food.

Tea-Smoked Fish

1 T. vegetable oil
¼ c. brown sugar
4 8- to 10-oz. fish steaks
1 tea-smoking base recipe (opposite)
4 bread slices

Combine oil and brown sugar. Rub fish steaks with oil and brown sugar mixture. Place in a sealable plastic bag and refrigerate for 2 to 3 hours to fuse flavors.

Heat an outdoor grill to high temperature. Place pan for smoking on grill. Add tea base. Heat until rice starts to smoke. Let smoke for 3 minutes.

While pan is heating, remove fish from plastic bag. Place each piece of fish on a slice of bread. Set on top of wire rack. Set wire rack inside smoking pan. Cover tightly with aluminum foil. Seal the foil as tightly to the pan as possible. Smoke for 3 minutes. Remove and keep covered. Set aside for 20 minutes. Remove rack and fish from pan. Prepare fish as desired or chill for future use.

Discard bread slices and rice.

Serves 4.

CHEF'S TIPS

• For scallops and shrimp with or without shells, lay 4 to 6 pieces on each bread slice and prepare as stated.

Grilled Fish Kabobs That Work

CHEF'S TIPS

• This recipe is easier than it looks and is a great way to serve a large gathering in short time.

• Firm-textured fish will stay on the skewer better than softer-textured fish.

• This recipe works because the vegetables are precooked.

• The bacon keeps the fish cubes moist.

• To "broom" green onions, remove the root end. Cut into 2-inch lengths. Cut lengthwise strips halfway down the green onion pieces. Place in ice water to curl strips.

16 fish cubes, cut into 1-inch squares
1 c. seasoned flour (see recipe p. 181)
8 strips bacon
1 qt. water for boiling vegetables
1 tsp. salt
8 small red potatoes
4 shallots, peeled
1 T. olive oil

2 large red peppers, cut into 8 cubes
2 zucchini, cut into 8 1/2-inch rounds
8 mushrooms, stems trimmed even to cap bottom
2 c. herbed dressing
1/2 c. dry sherry
2 lemons
4 long wooden or metal skewers
8 green onions, broomed

Cut fish into cubes and roll in seasoned flour in a pie plate. Remove to a rack and let dry for 10 minutes. Lay bacon out to warm up. In a saucepan, heat water and salt to boiling. Add red potatoes. Let boil for 10 minutes. Add whole shallots and boil for 5 minutes. Drain potatoes and shallots into a colander and let steam off. In a skillet, heat olive oil. Add pepper cubes, zucchini slices and mushroom caps and sauté for 2 minutes. Add sherry. Turn and simmer for 2 minutes more. Remove vegetables to a rack to cool. Wrap each fish cube with 1/2 piece bacon. Place on platter seam side down.

TO MAKE KABOB: Place a mushroom cap on one end of skewer, rounded side out. Next put on a zucchini slice, fish cube, pepper slice, fish cube, shallot, whole potato, shallot, fish cube, red pepper slice, fish cube and zucchini slice. Finish with mushroom, rounded side out.

Place the 4 kabobs in a long baking pan. Top with 2 c. herbed dressing. Cover with plastic wrap. Refrigerate for 1 hour or until needed.

TO GRILL: Heat grill medium-hot. Remove kabobs from pan. Let excess dressing run off. Place kabobs on grill until golden brown. Rotate a quarter turn at a time until all sides are golden brown. Check fish for doneness. Put on a platter. Place broomed green onion on end of each skewer.

Serves 4 to 6.

- Chicken breasts can be boiled with the potatoes and shallots. Chill breasts after cooking. Cut into pieces and add to the skewers.

Grilled Fish
Kabobs That Work

• This is one of those time-tested recipes that just cannot be beat!

• This recipe is perfect for a campfire. Use double foil and turn the fish pouches often. Keep on the medium-heat side of fire.

• When cutting carrots and zucchini, it is important to make pieces 1/2 to 1 inch thick and 3 to 4 inches long. This helps in the stacking.

Fish in a Tin Pouch

2 red peppers
4 8- to 10-oz. salmon or lake trout fillets or steaks
1 tsp. lemon pepper seasoning
4 large potatoes, unpeeled and sliced 1/2 inch thick
4 zucchini, sliced 1/2 inch thick into 3 long slabs
4 carrots, peeled and sliced 1/2 inch thick into 3 long slabs
2 large onions, sliced 1 inch thick
2 tsp. fresh thyme
4 tsp. fresh lemon juice
1/2 pound of butter, cut into 4 slabs

Preheat oven to 375°.

Cut peppers in half end to end. Remove seeds and stem. On a flat surface, lay out four large sheets of double-thick aluminum foil. In the center of each sheet, place a fish fillet. Season lightly with lemon pepper and top with potato slices, zucchini, carrots, onion slices, red peppers, thyme, lemon juice and a slab of butter.

Fold up foil to make a tight pouch, and bake in 375° oven for one hour. When carrots are tender, it is time to serve.

Serves 4.

NOTES

A Slimy Sandwich

I often joined my dad and his friends on fishing trips at local lakes. Dad's friend Russell was one of my favorites, but he had an annoying habit of bringing his own lunch then eating the lunches my mother made for my father and me.

We had a regimen. Dad sat in the back of the boat, ran the motor and fished out of the left side of the boat. Russell sat in the front of the boat and handled the anchor and the fish net. I sat in the middle of the boat, fished on the right side, put the fish on the stringer, gave bait to the guys, and passed out our lunches.

It was always the same routine. Fish for an hour or two and then eat lunch. This day, the Northern Pike were biting. I knew that as soon as things slowed down Russell would delve into the cooler, eat his own sandwich and then and take one of our sandwiches. This time I decided to teach him a lesson.

With my dad looking on, I unwrapped one of the sandwiches, picked out three of the biggest worms I could find from the bait box, placed them on a sandwich, re-wrapped it and put it back in the cooler under two of our sandwiches.

Sure enough, when the fish quit biting, Russell opened the cooler and ate his sandwich. My dad and I ate the next two sandwiches. Then Russell helped himself to one of our remaining sandwiches. My father and I smiled conspiratorially as Russell bit into the sandwich. A fat white worm hung from the corner of his mouth until, with a great slurp, it disappeared.

My dad exploded with laughter, fell off his seat into the bottom of the boat and let go of the motor. Russell began spitting and coughing. I broke into laughter as the boat started spinning around in a tight circle.

I learned several new words that day. After a while Russell forgave me, but from that day forward he always ate just his own sandwiches.

Baked & Roasted

CHEF'S TIPS

- Use cedar, oak or birch planks, 1 inch thick, 10 inches wide and 24 inches long.
- Be sure the plank is clean and free from splinters before heating. On the smooth side, spray with oil to coat. Place in a 375° oven for 20 minutes. Remove and top the plank smooth side with roasted fish.
- Don't be alarmed if the plank turns dark in color.

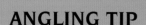

ANGLING TIP

Channel cats usually hold to deeper water during the day, and move to shallow areas at night to feed.

Roasted Fish on a Plank

6-lb. fish
1/2 c. butter, softened
1/8 tsp. white pepper
1 tsp. fresh thyme leaves, minced fine
1 T. cornstarch
1 tsp. fresh tarragon, minced fine
1 lemon for zest
2 c. seasoned flour (see recipe p. 181)

Preheat oven to 400°.

Remove all fish scales, clean inside cavity well and remove gills and eyes.

Combine soft butter with white pepper, thyme, cornstarch and tarragon. Brush a thick layer of butter mixture inside cavity. With a potato peeler, remove yellow skin from whole lemon in one piece Place lemon zest inside cavity. Brush both sides of fish with butter mixture and roll in flour. Place on a sheet of aluminum foil in a large baking pan. Roast fish in a 400° oven until skin is golden brown and meat is milky white. Remove from oven and mist with fresh lemon juice. Serve on a large, hot wooden plank.

Serves 4 to 6.

- *Roasting time for a 4- to 6-lb. fish is 25 minutes. Roasting time for a 6- to 8-lb. fish is 30 to 35 minutes.*

Italian Fish Bake

¼ c. olive oil
2 large boneless, skinless
fish fillets
½ c. seasoned flour
(see recipe p. 181)
2 T. olive oil
2 cloves garlic
1 c. red onion, diced into
½-inch pieces

1 c. red pepper, diced into
½-inch pieces
1 c. fresh mushrooms, sliced
into ¼-inch slices
½ c. dry red wine
½ c. black olive slices
1 T. fresh basil, chopped fine
1 qt. spaghetti sauce of choice
½ c. Parmesan cheese, freshly
shredded

Preheat oven to 375°.

Line a baking pan with aluminum foil. Brush with olive oil. Place one fish fillet skin side down on foil. Cut a slit in the center of the remaining fillet, leaving 2 inches on each end. Dust fillet with flour and place on top of first fillet. Spread the center open for addition of sauce.

To make sauce, heat a skillet with olive oil. Add garlic, onions and red pepper. Sauté until onion is tender. Add mushrooms and red wine. Bring to a boil. Add black olives, basil and spaghetti sauce. Simmer for 5 minutes on low heat.

Pour sauce over fish fillets. Sauce will overrun the pocket. Top with Parmesan cheese and bake at 375° for 25 to 30 minutes. Fish is ready when the fillets are flaky at the thickest part.

Serves 4.

- *Sometimes I make a pizza crust topped with slices of provolone cheese for the base. Bake a pizza crust golden brown. Cool and top with a layer of sliced provolone or mozzarella cheese. Place fish and sauce on top and bake as per recipe. (The reason for prebaking and topping crust with cheese is to keep the crust from becoming a soggy mess.)*

CHEF'S TIPS

• Most home chefs tend to overcook fish, so be careful.
• You can prepare sauce for fish a day in advance. Keep sauce separate from fish. Heat sauce and bake fish.
• Fish and sauce leftovers are great on hard rolls for sandwiches.

ANGLING TIP

Use large spoons or minnow-type lures along the edges of weed beds to catch pike.

CHEF'S TIPS

- Remove bones from ribs through the inside cavity, leaving the backbone intact to keep fish in one piece.
- A specific baking time cannot be given because each fish will cook differently
- A whole fish is a spectacular and ancient dish, naturally full of drama. This is your opportunity to impress your guests.

CHEF'S TIPS

- Add vinegar to the cleaning water; the acidity helps kill bacteria.
- Popcorn shrimp, crabmeat or scallop slices placed inside the fish rolls adds greatly to this dish.

Baked Stuffed Fish

1 whole fish, larger than 5 lbs.
salt and pepper to taste
3 c. cornbread, or fish and seafood stuffing
(see recipes p. 216 or p. 217)
2 c. tiny shrimp
1/4 c. melted butter

Preheat oven to 350°.

Clean and scale fish. Remove gills, eyes and dorsal fin. Place fish on a piece of double-thick aluminum foil. Salt and pepper cavity. Combine cornbread stuffing with tiny shrimp. Place inside fish cavity. Brush fish with butter. Fold sides of foil over head and tail and roll into a tight cylinder. Place on a large shallow baking pan, seam side down, and bake in a 350° oven until internal temperature is 160°. Use a meat thermometer to see if the fish is done.

Serves 4 to 6.

Onion Jumbos with Fish Roll-Ups

4 of the largest onions you can find
2 qts. water
1/3 c. cider vinegar
2 tsp. flour
2 tsp. Chef John's fish rub
(see recipe p. 183)

4 4- to 6-oz. boneless fillets
2 T. butter, softened
1 c. chicken or fish stock
(see recipe p. 47)

It makes no difference what color onions you use; only the size counts. Fill a large bowl half full of cold water and 1/3 cup cider vinegar. Gently plunge onions up and down to clean. Remove and set in a baking dish or Dutch oven stem end down. Cut 1/4 to 1/2 inch off the top. If onion will not sit up straight, tell their mothers or cut a very thin slice off the bottom. Remove centers of onions with a melon ball scoop or teaspoon, being careful to leave 1/4 inch thickness on sides and bottom.

Preheat oven to 375°.

Place flour and rub in a flat pan. Combine well. Coat each fish fillet in flour mixture. Do not shake off excess. Roll each fillet into a cylinder and place in the center of an onion. Top with soft butter. Place onion lid on top. Add chicken stock and onion pieces from centers to dish. Cover and bake at 375° for 45 minutes. Remove cover and bake for 10 minutes letting outside of onions get crisp. Gently remove and serve with polenta, risotto or spätzles.

Serves 4.

Baked Stuffed Fish

CHEF'S TIPS

- Toasted coconut and cashew pieces can be sprinkled over the top.
- For an attention-getter, cut butternut squash in half. Remove seeds. Brush with butter. Bake in a 375° oven for 45 minutes. When fish is done, place 1/2 cup rice in center and top with 2 fish roll-ups and sauce.

ANGLING TIP

By midsummer when the weather gets warm, walleyes seek cooler water and head to deeper parts of the lake.

Fish Roll-Up in Pear Plantain Orange Marmalade

8 6- to 8-oz. fish fillets,
at least 6 inches long
2 plantains or very green bananas
1 T. flour
1/2 tsp. lemon pepper
1 T. olive oil
1/3 c. red onion, diced into 1/4-inch cubes
1 T. lime juice
1 c. orange marmalade
2 tsp. cornstarch
1 c. fresh squeezed orange juice with pulp
2 T. fresh cilantro, chopped fine
2 ripe pears, peeled, seeded, cut into 1/4-inch slices

Preheat oven to 375°. Make sure to use fish fillets that are not too thick. Lay fish on a piece of aluminum foil, skin side down. Peel plantains. Cut into quarters. Place 2 plantain strips about 1/3 of the way up the fish fillet. Roll into a cylinder. Seal end with a pinch of flour and place in a baking dish, seal side down, with remaining plantain pieces. Sprinkle with lemon pepper.

In a skillet, heat oil. Add onion and cook until tender. Add lime juice and marmalade. Combine well and bring to a simmer. Dissolve cornstarch in orange juice and add to liquid. Whisk with a wire whisk until a smooth sauce is made. When sauce is clear and shiny, remove from heat. Add cilantro and pear slices. Pour over fish roll-ups. Cover and bake for 25 minutes in a 375° oven. The sauce should be thin. Place 2 pieces of fish on a mound of cooked white or wild rice for service.

Serves 4.

The Fisherman's Wife Pot Pie

1/4 c. butter
1/2 c. red onion, diced into 1/4-inch cubes
1 c. carrots, 1/4-inch-thick half-moons
1 c. potatoes, cut into 1/2-inch cubes
1/2 c. dry sherry wine
1/2 c. mushroom pieces, cut into 1/2-inch cubes
1 c. tomatoes, seeded and chopped into 1/2-inch pieces
1 c. fresh green beans, cut into 1-inch pieces
2 c. fish fillets, cut into 1-inch cubes
4 c. heavy cream
3 egg yolks
1/4 tsp. ground nutmeg
1/2 tsp. salt
1/4 tsp. white pepper
1 tsp. fresh thyme, or 1/2 tsp. dry thyme
2 tsp. fresh tarragon, or 1 tsp. dry tarragon
1/4 c. flour
1 pastry crust (see recipe p. 212)

Preheat oven to 350°.

Heat butter to a fast bubble in a skillet. Add onion and carrots and sauté for 3 minutes, stirring gently to keep from sticking. Add potato cubes and sherry, and simmer for 10 minutes on low. Remove from heat. Add mushrooms, tomatoes and green beans. Place mixture in a Dutch oven or large soufflé dish. Top with fish pieces. Place cream, egg yolks, nutmeg, salt, pepper, thyme, tarragon and flour in a bowl and combine to make a smooth sauce. Pour over fish.

Top with pastry crust. Seal crust to edges of dish. Cut a small hole in the center to let out steam. Brush crust evenly with cream to enhance browning. Bake at 350° for 1 hour.

Serves 4.

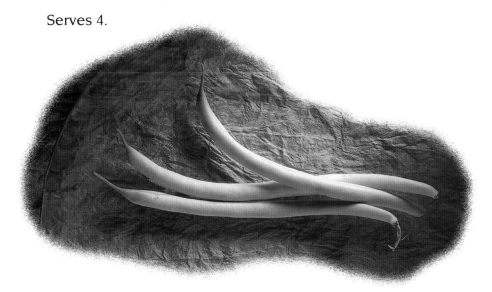

CHEF'S TIPS

- You may add different kinds of fish pieces, shrimp or scallops to this dish.
- Use heavy cream or the sauce will curdle.

ANGLING TIP

When fishing for bass, surface lures are most productive in shallow water (six feet and less).

Fish and Roasted Vegetable Napoleons

Fish and Roasted Vegetable Napoleons

1 large eggplant, cut into 8 slices
¼ c. olive oil
4 sweet potato slices, ¼ inch thick
4 red onion slices, ½ inch thick
4 zucchini slices, ¼ inch thick and 3 inches long
4 pineapple rings
4 jumbo-sized tomato slices, ½ inch thick
¼ tsp. salt
½ tsp. black pepper
1 tsp. dry thyme
8 2- to 3-oz. boneless fish fillets
1 T. flour
4 slices cheddar cheese
1 tsp. lemon pepper
4 slices mozzarella cheese
4 Anaheim or large jalapeño peppers
4 large sweet pickles
4 sprigs rosemary
1 extra-large lemon, cut into quarters

Preheat oven to 350°.

Wash all vegetables thoroughly. Slice eggplant and brush lightly with olive oil. Heat a large skillet. Add eggplant slices 4 at a time and sauté until golden brown on one side. Remove to a paper-towel-lined sheet pan, placing brown side down. Brush sweet potato slices with olive oil and sauté golden brown on both sides. Remove to sheet pan. Repeat with onions slices, zucchini slices and pineapple rings.

Slice tomatoes and season with salt, black pepper and thyme. Dredge fish in flour and sauté in 1 tablespoon olive oil until golden brown on both sides. Remove to paper-towel-lined platter.

To build Napoleons, cover a sheet pan with aluminum foil. Brush with olive oil. Build all four Napoleons one at a time. First, place a slice of eggplant brown side up. Top with a slice of cheddar cheese. Top with fish fillet. Sprinkle lemon pepper evenly over fish. Add zucchini slice, sweet potato slice, seasoned tomato slice, mozzarella cheese, fish fillet, pineapple ring and second eggplant slice, brown side down. Remove stem end and seeds from Anaheim pepper and stuff a sweet pickle inside pepper. Stick a sharp skewer through the stuffed Anaheim pepper and through the center of vegetable/fish stack. Place in a 350° oven for 25 minutes. Remove leaves from the bottom ¾ of the rosemary sprigs and sharpen the ends. Remove stacks from oven to warm plates. Replace skewers with rosemary sprigs. Serve with a lemon wedge.

Serves 4.

CHEF'S TIPS

- This recipe is fun to prepare.
- Use any vegetable or fruit of the season. Remember to precook them, as the time in the oven only heats the Napoleons through.
- You can substitute any mild or hot chili pepper for the Anaheim peppers.
- If sweet potatoes are not available, use any large potato slices.

ANGLING TIP

The best method for catching Chinook salmon in deep lakes is trolling with a plug or spoon. Use downriggers to get the lure down to where the fish are swimming.

CHEF'S TIPS

• Roast the squash until just tender. It will not bake further after adding the filling.

• Any medium-sized squash can be used in this recipe.

Spaghetti Squash Fish Boats

1 medium-large spaghetti squash
1/3 c. melted butter
1/2 c. onion, cut 1/4 inch thick
1/2 c. red pepper, cut 1/4 inch thick
2 c. sweet potatoes, diced into 1/4-inch pieces
1 c. mushrooms, cut 1/4 inch thick
2 c. broken fresh or frozen shrimp pieces
1/2 c. water chestnuts, drained and cut into quarters
1 tsp. fresh basil
1 tsp. fresh thyme
1 c. sweet and sour sauce
1 tsp. garlic salt
1/4 tsp. black pepper
2 c. fish, cut into 1-inch squares
1/2 c. cashew pieces

Preheat oven to 350°. Cut squash in half lengthwise. Scoop out seeds. Brush insides of squash lightly with butter and roast for 45 minutes at 350°.

While squash is roasting, heat remaining butter in a large skillet. Add onions, peppers and sweet potatoes. Cook for 4 minutes on medium heat. Add mushrooms, shrimp, water chestnuts, basil, thyme, sweet and sour sauce, garlic salt and pepper. Cook for 10 minutes, stirring well, and bring to a boil. Add fish and cover. Remove from heat and let steep for 5 minutes.

Fill squash halves with 1/2 vegetable/shrimp mixture. Place fish evenly over mixture. Top with remaining sauce. Sprinkle cashews evenly on top. Return to oven for 10 minutes. Serve with risotto, grits or cornbread.

Serves 4.

ANGLING TIP

In the evening during summer, walleyes come out of deeper water to patrol the shoreline for food.

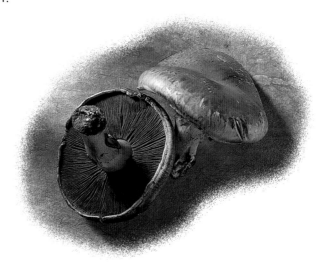

- This recipe works well with all fish steaks and fillets.
- For extra flavor, sprinkle with your favorite seasoning or seasoned salt when the fish comes out of the oven.

Coconut Pecan Trout

4 8- to 10-oz. trout, deboned, heads on
1/2 c. seasoned flour (see recipe p. 181)
1/2 c. pecan pieces
1 c. cereal flakes or granola
1/4 c. coconut flakes
1 c. egg wash (see recipe p. 181)
1/4 c. melted butter
1 lemon, cut into quarters

Preheat oven to 375°. Clean and debone trout. Place seasoned flour in a shallow pan. Combine pecans, cereal and coconut flakes in a shallow bowl. Coat fish with flour on both sides. Shake off excess. Place egg wash in another shallow pan and dip fish. Shake off extra eggs. Coat trout with pecan/coconut mixture on both sides, pressing firmly to make the breading stick.

Place on a buttered baking pan. Evenly pour melted butter over fish. Bake in a 375° oven for 15 minutes. Remove and splash with lemon juice.

Serves 4.

ANGLING TIP

Crankbaits: With northern pike, bigger lure equals bigger fish.

Fish, Potato and
Corn Muffins

Fish, Potato and Corn Muffins

4 c. white baking potatoes, sliced paper thin
12 boneless, skinless panfish fillets, cut into 2-inch pieces
1/2 c. cream
6 eggs
1 tsp. salt
1/4 tsp. white pepper
1/2 c. seasoned flour (see recipe p. 181)
1 c. whole-kernel corn, frozen
1 c. Farmer's cheese, grated
12 soda crackers, crumbled

Preheat oven to 375°.

The key to this recipe is slicing the potatoes thin enough. To achieve this, use a potato peeler, a sharp fillet knife (because the blade is thin), the slicing side of a box grater or a mandoline.

Cut twelve 5-inch-square pieces of aluminum foil. Spray a cupcake pan with vegetable oil. Place a foil piece in each hole and press to form a liner. Spray foil with vegetable oil. Place 2 to 3 slices of potato on the bottom and ring the walls with a double-thick layer of potato slices. Spray potatoes with vegetable oil. Press measuring cup on top of potato slices making a tight fit. Turn cup and gently remove. Place 2 pieces of fillet in each cup. Combine cream, eggs, salt, pepper, flour and corn and mix well. Add evenly over fillets in each potato crust. Top with grated cheese and cracker crumbs.

Bake at 375° for 20 to 25 minutes. When fillets are firm and pudding is thick and hot, remove from oven. Serve 2 to 3 muffins per person.

Serves 4 to 6.

CHEF'S TIPS

• This recipe is too much fun to skip, especially if you have children.
• For larger fillets, cut into pieces 1/2 inch thick and 1 inch square.
• These muffins are great for breakfast or an easy late supper.

ANGLING TIP

Lake trout tend to live in deeper water: Use lead-core line or down riggers to get your bait deep enough.

Fish-Stuffed Baked Potatoes

4 large baking potatoes
8 fish fillets
2 cans cream-style corn
1 c. seasoned flour
(see recipe p. 181)

⅓ c. oil
¼ c. butter
2 c. red onion, sliced
¼ inch thick
1 c. sour cream

Bake potatoes for 55 minutes in a 375° oven or roast in foil on the campfire until potatoes are just tender when lightly squeezed. While potatoes are baking, clean fish and heat cream-style corn hot.

Dredge fish fillets in seasoned flour and sauté golden brown on both sides in oil and butter. Remove fillets to paper-towel-lined bowl to keep hot. Add onions to butter and cook on low heat for 10 minutes. Turn often to keep sauté from burning.

Divide cooked onions among 4 plates. Top with a hot baked potato. Slice potato, making a pocket, and squeeze to open. Place ¼ of the corn in each potato. Top with 2 fish fillets and sour cream.

Serves 4.

Panfish Carrot Flan

¼ c. butter
1 c. carrots, peeled and coarsely grated
8 sunfish fillets, cut into 1-inch cubes
2 egg yolks
1½ c. heavy whipping cream
¼ tsp. salt
pinch white pepper
2 tsp. fresh tarragon, chopped fine
4 egg whites, room temperature
8 slices cheese croutons, cut into triangles (see recipe p. 218)

Preheat oven to 350°. Heat butter to a fast bubble in a medium skillet. Add grated carrots and sauté on low heat until carrots are tender. Add fish fillets. Cover and remove from heat. Let stand for 5 minutes. Remove cover and let it steam off.

In a large bowl, place egg yolks, heavy whipping cream, salt, pepper and tarragon. Whisk well to combine. When carrots and fish are at room temperature, add to egg mixture.

In a clean mixing bowl, add egg whites and beat to a light froth. (Do not overbeat.) Add to mixture and pour into soup cups or ramekins. Place in shallow baking pans. Add hot water ¾ of the way up the side of the soup cup. Place in a 350° oven for 25 minutes. Remove from oven and serve with cheese croutons.

Serves 4.

CHEF'S TIPS

- It is important to purchase the largest potatoes available.

CHEF'S TIPS

- Use a tender, light-flavored fish.
- Garnish with finely-diced sweet gherkin pickles and sour cream.

Fish Paprikosh

¼ c. whole butter
2 cloves garlic, minced
2 c. onion, diced into ½-inch pieces
1½ c. red peppers, cut into ½-inch cubes
¼ c. flour
1 T. paprika
1 tsp. salt
¼ tsp. white pepper
½ c. black olives, sliced ¼ inch thick
1 c. mushrooms, sliced ½ inch thick
1½ c. dry red wine
2 c. diced tomatoes and liquid
1 c. tomato puree
4 c. fish fillets, cut into 2-inch pieces
1 c. sour cream and chopped parsley for garnish

Preheat oven to 350°.

Heat butter in a Dutch oven to a fast bubble. Add garlic, onion and red peppers and sauté until onions are tender. Combine flour, paprika, salt and white pepper. Add to onions and mix smooth with a wooden spoon. Add olives, mushrooms, wine, diced tomatoes and liquid and tomato puree. Bring to a boil. Simmer base for 15 minutes on low heat. Place fish on top of base. Cover and bake in a 350° oven for 20 minutes. Stir gently and serve. Top with sour cream and chopped parsley.

Serves 4 to 6.

CHEF'S TIPS

• Do not overcook fish, as it will turn in-to a watery, crumbly mush.

ANGLING TIP

When fishing for panfish, slip bobber rigs are great for keeping the bait at the correct depth. Perch often stay near the bottom of the lake, feeding on snails and other organisms on rocks or in the mud.

Pike St. Jacques in Portabella Mushrooms

Pike St. Jacques in Portabella Mushrooms

Sauce

2 T. clarified butter
1/2 c. shallots, chopped into
1/4-inch pieces
1 clove garlic, minced fine
1 c. fresh crimini mushrooms,
sliced 1/4 inch thick
2 T. flour
1/2 tsp. salt
1/8 tsp. white pepper
1/4 tsp. dry mustard
1/2 tsp. fresh lemon juice
1 c. dry white wine
1/2 tsp. Worcestershire sauce
4 egg yolks
1 c. heavy cream

To Prepare Mushrooms

4 large portabella mushrooms
2 T. clarified butter
(see recipe p. 189)
1/2 c. dry sherry wine

To Prepare Fish

12 boneless, skinless pike
pieces, cut into 2-inch squares
1 c. seasoned flour
(see recipe p. 181)
1/4 c. clarified butter
(see recipe p. 189)
4 c. country mashed potatoes
(see recipe p. 205)
1/2 c. Parmesan cheese, grated

CHEF'S TIPS

- This is a variation of the classic Coquilles St. Jacques recipe.
- Any white boneless fish works equally well. You may also make this recipe with scallops or a scallop and fish combination.
- If you do not have a pastry bag and star tube, place the potato mixture in a medium-sized sealable plastic bag. Cut a small piece off one corner and squeeze a potato border on the plate. Dip a salad fork in melted butter and mark the top of the potato border.
- As an appetizer, serve in smaller bowls.

Make country mashed potatoes. Preheat oven to 400°.

For sauce, put 2 tablespoons clarified butter in a skillet and heat until it bubbles. Add shallots. Cook until clear and tender. (Do not brown.) Add garlic and mushrooms. Stir gently. Simmer for 2 minutes. Combine flour, salt, pepper and dry mustard. Sprinkle evenly over sauce. Very gently swirl and stir flour into vegetables. When lumps are gone, add lemon juice, white wine and Worcestershire sauce. Simmer on low heat for 3 to 4 minutes. Combine egg yolks and cream in a bowl. Slowly add 1/2 cup hot wine liquid from base to egg/cream mixture to temper. Combine and slowly add to skillet. Stir with a wooden spoon to make a smooth rich sauce. Remove from heat and cover.

To prepare portabella mushrooms, remove stems and wash mushrooms. In a large sauté pan, heat 2 tablespoons clarified butter. Add mushrooms top side down. Sauté 1 minute. Turn caps. Add 1/2 cup sherry wine and simmer for 3 minutes. Remove caps and hold for service.

To prepare fish, dredge fillets in seasoned flour. Shake off excess. Heat a skillet with clarified butter on medium heat. Add fish pieces. Sauté 1 minute. Turn and repeat. Remove from heat.

To assemble four portions, place portabella mushroom caps inside up on a baking pan. Using a pastry bag with a large star tube, pipe out a thick border of mashed potatoes around the rim of each Portabella mushroom. Place 3 pieces of pike in the center of mushroom. Top with 1/4 sauce. Sprinkle Parmesan cheese evenly over the top. Place in a 400° oven until cheese is melted and potatoes are light brown. Remove with hot pads. Serve.

Serves 4.

CHEF'S TIPS

• This is my interpretation of paella. True paella uses mussels, lobster or squid. Put them in the recipe if available.

• This is a participation cooking event. The more helpers, the better.

ANGLING TIP

Walleyes love a weed bed where they can hide and grab passing baitfish. Cast your lure and retrieve it along a well-defined edge for an irresistible presentation.

Fish Paella

8 chicken leg and thigh quarters
4 red peppers, seeded and cut into quarter wedges
4 plum tomatoes, cut in half
1 c. whole stuffed Spanish olives (medium size)
1 c. whole black olives
2 c. whole artichoke hearts, fresh or canned
2 large red onions, cut into quarter wedges
1 c. olive oil
4 cloves garlic, cut in half

8 smoked pork chops
1 c. butter
1 1/2 lbs. long-grain rice, uncooked
2 tsp. salt
1/2 tsp. black pepper
1 T. Spanish paprika
20 saffron threads
2 c. green peas, fresh or frozen
2 lbs. shrimp, shells on
1 qt. clam broth
8 8- to 10-oz. boneless fish fillets, skins on

Preheat oven to 375°.

Paella can be made in any large skillet. A paella pan is wide and shallow with two handles. It is made from cast iron, steel or copper. It can be found in specialty shops.

The most important part of recipe preparation is getting all of the ingredients ready. This is a must before you start this paella dish.

Clean chicken pieces, removing extra fat, skin and pin feathers. Remove stem end and seeds from peppers. Cut peppers into 4 wedges. Remove end of tomatoes and cut in half. Drain liquid from olives and artichoke hearts. Peel onions. Remove stem end and cut into 4 wedges.

In a large paella pan or iron skillet, heat olive oil hot. Add chicken and brown on both sides. Fry for 15 minutes on medium heat, being careful not to burn. Push chicken to one side. Add garlic and onions and cook until onions are clear and tender. Push to one side and stack chicken quarters on top. Add pork chops and fry light brown on both sides. With a skimmer, lift all ingredients from the oil. Place on a pan and set aside for a few minutes.

Add butter to oil and bring to a fast bubble. Add red pepper and artichoke hearts. Sauté for 2 minutes. Add rice. Combine well with a wooden spoon. Simmer for 15 minutes. Combine salt, pepper, paprika and saffron threads. Mix well to remove lumps from paprika. Sprinkle over rice mixture.

Add tomato halves, skin side down, and olives. Add peas evenly over mix. Place chops and chicken pieces alternately around the sides with vegetables and liquid. Add shrimp and clam broth. Place onions in center and cover with fish fillets. Return liquid to a boil and let simmer for 5 minutes. Place in a 375° oven for 20 minutes. When rice is cooked, remove to center of table on a hot plate. Let everyone serve themselves.

Serves 6 to 8.

Fish Paella

CHEF'S TIPS

• Do not overblanch asparagus and carrots. Chill them in ice water immediately and remove as soon as they are cold.

• When poaching fish roll-ups, remember that the vegetables are already cooked. When the fish is tender, the vegetables will be hot.

• To create pepper strips, set a pepper stem end up. Remove the stem and slice across the whole pepper, making horseshoe strips 1/2 inch wide. The end pieces may be poached and served.

ANGLING TIP

Watch the moon: Feeding activity for walleyes increases during the days surrounding new and full moons.

Poached Fish Roll-Ups with Asparagus and Carrots

2 c. cold water
1/2 c. dry white wine
1/2 tsp. salt
8 whole cloves stuck into outside of a whole lemon
12 large asparagus spears, cut in half
8 carrot strips, 1/3 inch thick and 3 inches long
4 8- to 10-oz. boneless fish fillets
2 large yellow peppers, cut into 1/2-inch strips
1 c. chicken stock (see recipe p. 47)
4 c. rice pilaf (see recipe p. 208)

In a large saucepot, heat water, wine, salt and lemon to a brisk boil. Add asparagus and carrot strips and return water to a boil. With a skimmer, remove vegetables immediately and plunge into ice water to stop the cooking process. Keep vegetable liquid.

When vegetables are well chilled, roll 4 asparagus pieces and 3 carrot pieces in fillets, skin side out. Wrap two 1/2-inch-thick strips of yellow pepper around outside of fish roll. Fasten with a long toothpick. Place fish roll-up seam side down in vegetable liquid. Cover and simmer on low for 15 minutes.

Remove pot from heat. Test for doneness. When fish is tender, remove from broth with a slotted spoon. Serve fish on steamed or fried rice, seam side down.

Serves 4.

**Poached Fish Roll-Ups with
Asparagus and Carrots**

CHEF'S TIPS

- Other cheeses may be used in place of Swiss cheese.
- For extra spiciness, add roasted green chili peppers to the crab meat.
- Imitation crab can be substituted for crab meat.

Fish Cordon Bleu

8 4- to 6-oz. fish fillets, cut 1 inch thick
1 c. seasoned flour (see recipe p. 181)
½ tsp. black pepper
8 thin slices Swiss cheese
1 c. crab meat
1 c. fresh whole wheat bread crumbs (see recipe p. 181)
½ c. freshly grated Parmesan cheese
1 c. egg wash (see recipe p. 181)
⅓ c. clarified butter (see recipe p. 189)
1 c. ivory caper sauce (see recipe p. 172)
1 lemon, cut into 4 wedges

Preheat oven to 350°.

Dredge fish fillets in seasoned flour and lay on a cutting board. Sprinkle black pepper over the fillets and gently press into the surface of the fish. On all fish fillets, place a piece of Swiss cheese which is slightly smaller than the fillet.

On four fish fillets, place ¼ cup crab meat atop the Swiss cheese. Cover each of the four crab-topped fish fillets with one of the cheese-topped fillets forming four sandwiches.

Combine bread crumbs and Parmesan cheese in a pie pan and set aside. Dredge each sandwich in seasoned flour. Shake off excess flour and press around the edges to make a seal. Dip in egg wash. Dredge in the bread crumb/ Parmesan cheese mixture. Coat well, making sure there are no bare spots.

Heat clarified butter in an ovenproof skillet. Sauté the four fish sandwiches until golden brown on both sides. Cover skillet and place in oven. Bake for 15 minutes. Serve with ivory caper sauce and lemon wedges.

Serves 4.

Fish and Seafood Strudel

1 T. cornstarch
8 sheets frozen phyllo pastry, 14 inches long and 12 inches wide, thawed (see recipe p. 214)
½ c. melted butter
2 c. risotto, room temperature (see recipe p. 209)
¼ c. pine nuts or almond slices
1 T. fresh thyme, or 1 tsp. dry thyme
½ c. fresh white bread crumbs (see recipe p. 181)
1 tsp. fresh lemon juice
1 c. boneless, skinless fish, diced ½ inch wide and no longer than 3 inches
1 c. scallops, crab meat or cooked shrimp
½ c. tartar sauce (see recipe p. 171)
1 egg, beaten
1 T. milk

Preheat oven to 350°.

On a cotton pastry cloth or dish towel, spread 1 tablespoon cornstarch to keep phyllo sheets from sticking. Lay a phyllo sheet out flat. Brush with melted butter. Top with second sheet. Repeat until all 8 sheets are in an even stack.

Combine risotto, pine nuts, thyme and bread crumbs. Gently and evenly spread over dough. Use the back side of a large spoon for spreading mixture. Sprinkle lemon juice over fish and place in a line 3 inches from the top of the dough. Place a line of seafood halfway down the filling. Top with tartar sauce.

With a soft pastry brush, apply a thin coat of egg wash to sides and bottom of dough. Fold sides of dough over filling gently. Start at the top and roll toward you like a jelly roll. Before the last rotation, dust off cornstarch with a soft brush or cloth to help make a better seal on the bottom. Spread tartar sauce over phyllo sheets except for 1 inch on the sides and 2 inches on the bottom.

Lightly grease a baking pan. Place pan next to work surface and pull pastry towel to edge. Gently roll strudel over pan. Arrange strudel so seam side is down. Brush off excess cornstarch. Add 1 tablespoon milk to beaten eggs and evenly brush strudel with a thin coat of egg wash. With a thin wooden pick or skewer, put 3 to 4 holes in strudel to let steam out.

Place in a 350° oven for 25 to 30 minutes. Remove and let sit 5 minutes and cut into 2-inch-thick pieces.

Serves 4.

CHEF'S TIPS

• If you want to make strudel in advance, bake and keep it in the refrigerator. To serve, reheat in a 300° oven for 5 to 7 minutes or on a defrost cycle in the microwave for 1 to 2 minutes.

• Strudel is excellent whether eaten hot or cold.

• All kinds of seafood and fish are great in this recipe.

• Remember to keep fish pieces small and flat.

ANGLING TIP

Medium- or medium-heavy-action rods are best for jig-fishing walleyes.

CHEF'S TIPS

- Green peppers can be used in place of red peppers.
- I was a cook and baker on a submarine in the Navy, so if it looked like a bag, it must be a sea bag!

ANGLING TIP

Northern pike thrive in cool water. The best times to fish for pike are late spring and early summer, late summer and early fall, and in winter just after ice forms on the lakes.

Fish in a Red Sea Bag

4 4- to 6-oz. fish fillets
2 tsp. Cajun seasoning
4 slices provolone or Swiss cheese
4 ham slices, 1/8 inch thick
4 large red peppers
2 tsp. olive oil
1 c. red onion, diced into 1/4-inch pieces

1 c. chicken stock (see recipe p. 47)
1 c. mustard pretzel crumbs
1 green pepper, diced into 1/4-inch pieces
1 c. carrots, diced into 1/4-inch pieces
1/4 tsp. black pepper

Preheat oven to 350°.

Sprinkle fish fillets with Cajun seasoning and top with a slice of Provolone cheese and ham. Roll up into cylinders. Set aside.

Remove the tops and seeds of the red peppers. Set tops aside. Place one fish fillet cylinder in each red pepper. Top with 1/2 teaspoon olive oil. In between fish cylinder and pepper, put red onion pieces to fill pepper. Top with chicken stock and pretzel crumbs.

Place remaining red onion pieces, green pepper, carrots and red pepper pieces on the bottom of a casserole dish. Place filled red peppers on vegetables. Cover and bake in a 350° oven for 1 1/2 hours. When fish is tender, remove from oven. Serve with vegetables and liquid from casserole.

Serves 4.

Fish in a Red Sea Bag

CHEF'S TIPS

•It is important to purchase the largest potatoes available.

•Slice potatoes with a mandoline or the slicing end of a box grater. A sharp potato peeler also works well. This is well worth the potato-slicing time.

•This works with all fish fillets no longer than 10 inches or thicker than 1 inch.

ANGLING TIP

Spin casting with light tackle and small, shiny lures is an effective method for catching brook trout.

Rainbow Trout in Salt-Crusted Balsamic Potato Crust

2 large white baking potatoes	1 c. butter, softened
2 T. balsamic vinegar	8 4- to 6-oz. rainbow trout
2 T. fresh orange juice	fillets
olive oil spray	kosher salt

To prepare potato crust, peel potatoes and slice paper-thin, making as large a slice as possible. In a glass baking dish, place potato slices, balsamic vinegar and orange juice. Let stand at room temperature for 10 to 15 minutes.

On a flat surface, lay 4 sheets of plastic wrap, 12 inches long and 10 inches wide. Spray with olive oil. Place a double layer of potato slices overlapping each other on each sheet of wrap. The overlapping is important. Brush with soft butter. Place a fish fillet, skin side down, in the center of the potatoes. Brush with butter and top with a second matching fillet, skin side up. To cover the fish with the potato crust, lift the plastic wrap underneath the potatoes. Roll as tightly as possible without breaking the crust. Place on a flat pan and chill for at least 1 hour in refrigerator.

To cook, carefully remove plastic wrap by unrolling or cutting with a very sharp knife. The potatoes will be a dark brown from the balsamic vinegar. Brush outside with soft butter and evenly sprinkle with kosher salt. Place 8 inches from heat source in oven and broil until potatoes are golden brown. Gently turn with a large spatula. Sprinkle top with kosher salt and broil until golden brown. Turn off broiler immediately. Leave fish in oven for 10 more minutes. Remove from oven and serve with grilled vegetables.

Serves 4.

Trout en Papillote

4 10- to 12-oz. whole trout, cleaned
4 sheets brown paper or parchment paper
1 tsp. lemon pepper
¼ c. butter
1 tsp. fresh thyme
2 tsp. fresh lemon juice

Preheat oven to 375°.

Clean and remove gills from trout, leaving the head, tail and fins on. Wash out cavity. Cut a piece of clean brown paper 14 inches wide and 18 inches long. Lay paper out flat and brush with soft butter. Place fish on top of paper and season inside and out with lemon pepper. Place 2 teaspoons butter, thyme and lemon juice in cavity and fold fish in paper by folding sides over head and tail and rolling up the remaining sides tightly around fish body.

Set fish on baking pan, seam side down. Bake in 375° oven for 15 to 20 minutes. To serve, cut a slit in paper and serve open.

Serves 4.

- You may use other boneless fish fillets, such as small pike, salmon and lake trout.

CHEF'S TIPS

- This is an elegant way to prepare fish ... and an exceptionally easy recipe!
- Use brown paper from a roll or cut a large, clean brown paper bag into squares.
- Use kitchen parchment paper in place of brown paper if desired. Do not use plastic food film or wax paper as it will melt.

CHEF'S TIPS

• You can also make this over a campfire. When cooking over a campfire, add 1/2 cup extra stock to keep the potatoes from sticking to the pan.

• A teaspoon of your favorite salad dressing over the fish fillets adds a great flavor.

Baked Fish and Camp Potatoes

1/4 c. butter
1 c. onion, sliced 1/4 inch thick
1/4 c. flour
1/2 tsp. salt
1/8 tsp. black pepper
3 c. potatoes, sliced 1/4 inch thick, skins on
1/2 c. barbeque sauce of choice
1 cup chicken stock (see recipe p. 47)
4 4- to 6-oz. fish fillets
2 tsp. lemon juice

Preheat oven to 375°.

Heat butter in a Dutch oven. Add onions and sauté until tender. Add flour, salt, pepper and stir to combine. Add potatoes, barbeque sauce and chicken stock. Cover and bake at 375° for 45 minutes. Remove cover. Add fish fillets. Sprinkle with lemon juice. Cover and bake 15 minutes and serve.

Serves 4.

CHEF'S TIPS

• The thicker the fish steak or fillet, the better. If using a tender fillet, place potatoes on the bottom of the stack first.

Scout Camp Fish Bake

4 carrots, sliced 1/2 inch thick, 4 inches long
2 large onions, sliced 1/2 inch thick
2 red peppers, cut in half, seeded and stemmed
2 large Idaho potatoes, sliced 1/2 inch thick, unpeeled
4 zucchini, sliced 1/2 inch thick, 4 inches long
4 8- to 10-oz. fish steaks or slabs
1 tsp. dry thyme
1 T. lemon pepper
1/2 lb. butter
1 T. fresh lemon juice

Lay four large sheets of double-thick aluminum foil on a flat surface. Peel carrots and onions. Remove seeds from peppers and slice vegetables.

To build each fish bake, place a fish steak in the center of each foil sheet. Top with 2 potato slices, 2 zucchini slices, 2 carrot slices, 1 onion slice, half red pepper. Sprinkle with thyme and lemon pepper. Top with a thick slice of butter and sprinkle with lemon juice.

Fold up foil to make a tight pouch. Place on medium-heat side of campfire or grill. Turn often to roast evenly. It takes about 30 minutes. (Or bake in a 375° oven for 1 hour.)

Serves 4.

CHEF'S TIPS

- I use a roasting bag in a Dutch oven for camp cooking.
- The vegetables need to be cubed small to be tender when fish are done.
- The liquid from vegetables and fish makes the sauce.

The Fish Is in the Bag

4 8- to 10-oz. fish fillets
1/2 c. instant potatoes
1/2 c. Parmesan cheese, grated
2 tsp. fresh thyme
1 tsp. salt
1/8 tsp. white pepper
medium to large oven bag
2 c. diced potatoes, skins on

1 c. red onion, diced into
1/4-inch cubes
1 c. carrots, diced into
1/4-inch cubes
1 c. celery, peeled and diced
into 1/4-inch cubes
2 tsp. lemon juice
1 1/2 T. butter, melted

Preheat oven to 375°. Cut fish fillets into 1 1/2 inch cubes. Combine instant potatoes, Parmesan cheese, thyme, salt and pepper together in a shallow bowl and toss gently. Put fish in mixture and coat.

Place diced vegetables, lemon juice and melted butter in an oven bag. Shake gently to combine. Remove fillets from dry mixture. Add remaining dry ingredients to vegetable bag and gently toss again. Place bag in a baking pan or Dutch oven. Top the vegetable mixture with fish. Close bag and fasten tight. Put a slit in the top of the bag and bake at 375° for 20 minutes. Remove from oven and serve.

Serves 4.

- If you have the time, homemade crust is always best.

Fish Calzone

1 T. olive oil
2 cloves garlic, minced
1/2 c. celery, diced into 1/4-inch pieces
1/2 c. onion, cut into 1/4-inch cubes
2 c. fish fillets, cut into 1-inch-wide slices
1 T. flour
1/4 tsp. black pepper
1/2 tsp. salt
2 tsp. fennel seeds
1/4 c. dry red wine
1 c. plum tomatoes, cut into 1/2-inch cubes
1 T. fresh basil, chopped coarse
1 c. crimini mushrooms, sliced 1/4 inch thick
1/2 c. Canadian bacon, cut into 1/2-inch squares
2 c. mozzarella cheese, shredded
1 tube refrigerated pizza crust
1/2 c. egg wash (see recipe p. 181)
2 T. cornmeal

Preheat oven to 375°. Heat olive oil in a skillet. Add garlic, celery and onions and sauté until onions are clear and tender. Add fish. Combine flour, black pepper, salt and fennel seeds in a bowl. Gently sprinkle over fish mixture. Stir to combine. Add red wine, tomatoes, basil, mushrooms, Canadian bacon and shredded cheese. Toss to combine well. Place filling in a bowl and let cool.

One pizza crust makes two calzones. On a flour-dusted baking cloth, roll out crust 1/4 inch thick. Cut in half. Brush with egg wash. Place 1/2 of the filling in center of each dough piece. Fold crust to make an envelope. Seal by pressing a fork around the edges. Sprinkle cornmeal on a large baking sheet. Place calzones on baking sheet. Brush lightly with egg wash. Poke 2 holes on top of each calzone with a knife tip for steam to escape. Bake in a 375° oven for 20 to 25 minutes. Serve with spaghetti sauce or salsa.

Serves 2.

NOTES

STRIPER FISHING AT MARTHA'S VINEYARD

My Grandpa Archie was a Norwegian-American, rural Minnesotan who loved to read about far-away places. When I was six years old, he shared his collection of National Geographic Magazines with me. In one issue, there was a story about fishing on Cape Cod using long rods. This was exotic and intriguing for a young, mid-western farm boy and became one of the first of many things placed on my wish list.

Many decades later my son Carlton helped me fulfill that wish. A resident of New Hampshire, Carlton worked in the fishing industry in New England and had contacts on Martha's Vineyard. He invited me to go false albacore tuna and striped bass fishing with him.

We took the ferry to the island and stayed in a small, rustic cabin. The first day we fished for false albacore tuna fish. They streak across the water looking for baitfish. To land one the wind must be tested, their speed guessed and the line cast in front of the fish. It is no easy task.

I used my trusty, light spinning rod and Carlton used his fly rod. He caught the first fish. It was all bone and muscle and put up a terrific fight. As soon as the pictures were taken, Carlton released the fish back into the ocean.

After countless casts, I hooked one of those streaking torpedoes. It was a 20 minute fight and I was sure the fish weighed at least 35 pounds. Imagine my surprise when it turned out to be a 7-pounder! I needed a rest and some lunch.

After lunch and a short nap, it was off to the north side of the island to fish for striped bass. The wind had picked up and it was overcast and misting. Donning stocking caps and raincoats, we prepared to fish. Carlton supplied ocean rods and reels, along with various colored plugs. We had also had stocked up on eels, a special treat for striped bass. We strapped on headlamps as the night closed in.

Within minutes the stripers began to hit. Most were in the five to seven pound range. The highlight of the night was when we both had fish on our lines at the same time. We each caught at least a dozen fish before the adventure was over.

As the waves crashed and the fish bit, no words were needed. We both kept one fish and I got to have my great striper adventure. Grandpa Archie would have been pleased.

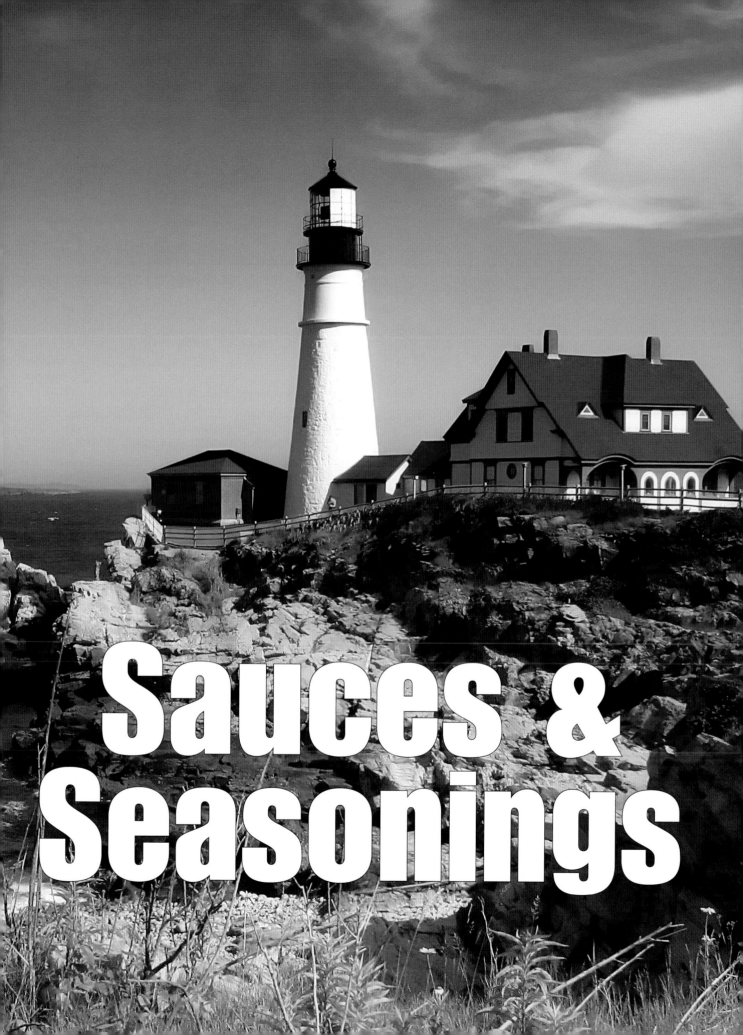

Sauces & Seasonings

SAUCES

Cocktail Sauce

½ c. horseradish, well
drained
1 c. tomato catsup
1 c. chili sauce
½ tsp. black pepper

1 T. lemon juice
3 drops Tabasco sauce
1 tsp. Worcestershire sauce
½ tsp. onion salt

Put horseradish in a strainer and let dry. Mix all ingredients thoroughly in a bowl. Place in a covered glass container and keep refrigerated.

ANGLING TIP

Catfish under ten pounds are best for eating. Release of trophy catfish is encouraged, as it can take 20 years or more for the fish to reach that size. Trophy blue catfish have been weighed at 120 pounds, flatheads of 150 pounds have been reported, and channel cats over 40 pounds are not uncommon in some parts of the United States.

Tartar Sauce

¾ c. dill pickles, diced into ¼-inch pieces
⅓ c. onion, diced into ¼-inch pieces
¾ c. black olives, diced into ¼-inch pieces
1 c. mayonnaise
1 c. sour cream
1 T. sugar
1 T. fresh lemon juice
4 drops Tabasco sauce
1 tsp. coarse-ground black pepper
2 tsp. Worcestershire sauce

Dice crisp dill pickles, onion and black olives. Place in a strainer and gently press mixture to remove excess liquid.

In a mixing bowl, place mayonnaise, sour cream, sugar, lemon juice, Tabasco, pepper and Worcestershire sauce and mix well. Add onions, pickles and black olives and gentvly fold in.

Remove from bowl and keep covered in refrigerator up to one week.

Fish Velouté

3 c. double-strength fish stock (see recipe p. 47)
1 c. half-and-half
½ c. dry white wine
1 c. roux (see recipe p. 180)

In a saucepan heat stock, half-and-half and wine. Whisk in roux slowly to make a smooth sauce. Simmer on low heat for 20 minutes. Stir with a wooden spoon from time to time, making sure bottom of pan is not scorching.

Remove from heat and put through a strainer or blend in a blender for a smooth, lump-free consistency.

Makes 1 quart.

CHEF'S TIPS
- You can substitute green olives stuffed with pimientos for the black olives.
- It is important to strain olives, pickles and onions well.

CHEF'S TIPS
- Simmer sauce just below its boiling point.
- If fish stock is not available, use chicken stock or clam broth.

CHEF'S TIPS

- Do not reduce the liquid in the first stages of preparing this sauce.
- Serve the sauce as soon as possible after preparing.
- For a richer flavor and color, add 2 tablespoons fresh fish roe after the cream is thick.

Ivory Caper Sauce

1½ T. butter
¼ c. shallots, diced into ¼-inch pieces
1 T. flour
1 tsp. lemon juice
⅓ c. dry white wine
1 pinch white pepper
1 large bay leaf
¼ c. capers
½ c. heavy cream

Melt butter in a sauté pan. Add shallots and sauté until clear. Add flour and reduce heat to medium. Cook for 2 minutes, stirring with a wooden spoon. Add lemon juice, white wine, pepper and bay leaf and simmer for 5 minutes on low heat. Do not boil. Remove bay leaf and add capers and cream. Simmer until cream thickens and serve.

Red Wine Barbeque Demi-Glace

1 qt. burgundy table wine
1 pt. barbeque sauce
2 tsp. lemon juice
½ tsp. white pepper

In a heavy saucepot over high heat, reduce volume of red wine to 1 cup. Add barbeque sauce, lemon juice and white pepper. Bring to a simmer on low heat for 5 minutes. Remove and place in a covered container and refrigerate.

CHEF'S TIPS

- Please do not share this recipe with your friends. It is our secret!

Mustard-Dill Sour Cream Sauce

1 tsp. olive oil
2 T. shallots, diced into
1/4-inch pieces
1 clove garlic, minced fine
1 T. Dijon mustard
2 tsp. spicy German mustard
1/2 c. sour cream

1/4 c. chicken stock
(see recipe p. 47)
1 tsp. cornstarch
1/4 tsp. dry mustard
1/8 tsp. black pepper
2 tsp. fresh dill weed,
minced coarse

Heat olive oil in a saucepan until hot. Add shallots and garlic and cook until shallots are transparent and tender. Put mustards, sour cream, chicken stock, cornstarch, dry mustard and pepper in a blender and puree smooth. Add slowly to shallots. Add dill weed and stir with a wooden spoon to keep from sticking. Simmer until sauce has a shiny, clear appearance.

Place in a bowl. Cover and keep warm until service.

CHEF'S TIPS

• Mustard sauce is also excellent cold.

• To store, keep in a covered container in refrigerator.

Béarnaise Sauce

1/4 c. shallots, diced into
1/4-inch pieces
1 T. crushed peppercorns
1 c. tarragon vinegar

hollandaise sauce
(see recipe p. 179)
1 tsp. tarragon leaves

Place shallots, peppercorns and tarragon vinegar in a small frying pan and simmer on low heat until liquid is almost evaporated. Place in a cheesecloth or dish towel and squeeze out all the liquid. Resulting béarnaise base should be 1 to 2 teaspoons.

Now prepare hollandaise sauce but substitute béarnaise base for lemon juice and Tabasco sauce. Add tarragon leaves, stir in sauce and serve.

CHEF'S TIPS

• If tarragon vinegar is not available, use white vinegar with 1 tablespoon dry tarragon leaves.

CHEF'S TIPS

• To turn up the heat, add hotter chili peppers, or leave the pepper seeds in.

Chili Pepper Tartar Sauce

tartar sauce (see recipe p. 171)
2 jalapeño peppers, diced into ¼-inch pieces
1 tsp. tarragon leaves

Prepare a single batch of tartar sauce. Remove seeds, white membrane and stem from jalapeño peppers. Dice into ¼-inch pieces. Add peppers and tarragon leaves to tartar sauce. Mix and refrigerate.

CHEF'S TIPS

• The most important detail in making mushroom sauce is to use fresh mushrooms.

• Wild forest mushrooms have more flavor than the domestic button mushrooms.

• If fish velouté is not available or you are pressed for time, use a prepared gravy of your choice.

Mushroom Sauce

1 T. butter
¼ c. shallots, diced into ¼-inch pieces
3 c. fresh mushrooms, sliced
1 c. dry sherry
3 c. fish velouté (see recipe p. 171)

In a sauté pan, heat butter. Add shallots and sauté until transparent. Add mushrooms and toss lightly for 20 seconds. Add sherry and simmer for 3 minutes. Add velouté and bring to a boil. Reduce heat and simmer for 10 minutes before serving.

Herbed Cream Sauce

2 T. herbed dressing
1/3 c. shallots, diced into
1/4-inch pieces
2 cloves garlic, minced fine
1 c. buttermilk
1/4 c. flour

1/8 tsp. freshly ground white
pepper
2 T. fresh tarragon
2 tsp. fresh thyme
1/2 tsp. dry oregano
1 c. heavy cream

Heat herbed dressing to a bubble in a saucepot. Add shallots and garlic and simmer for 10 minutes. Combine buttermilk and flour to make a smooth, thin paste. Add to shallots. Stir with a wooden spoon to make a thick base. Add seasonings and cream. Simmer on low heat for 8 minutes, stirring often to prevent scorching. Sauce should be smooth and tangy.

Horseradish Sauce

1/2 c. horseradish, well drained
1/2 tsp. Worcestershire sauce
1 1/2 c. mayonnaise
3 T. sugar
4 drops Tabasco sauce

Place horseradish in a fine strainer and press out liquid until almost dry. Place all ingredients in a mixing bowl and mix well. Keep in a covered glass container and refrigerate.

Makes 2 cups.

CHEF'S TIPS

• If buttermilk is not available, substitute 1 cup whole milk and 1 tablespoon cider vinegar.

ANGLING TIP

Use light tackle when fishing for crappies. Their mouth is surrounded by a paper-thin membrane, which tears easily.

• The best caviar is Beluga, osetra or sevruga. It is very expensive and, in reality, lumpfish caviar will suffice.

Ivory Tarragon Caviar Sauce

1 1/2 c. leeks cut in half and sliced 1/4 inch thick2 T. butter
1/2 c. dry white wine
2 tsp. honey
1/8 tsp. freshly ground white pepper

1 T. fresh tarragon leaves, minced medium
1 c. sour cream, room temperature
1 oz. black caviar

Before using, trim leek rootlets and leaf ends down to within 1 inch of where the white part starts. Split in half and wash. Lay halves flat and cut into 1/4-inch-wide slices.

In a medium skillet, heat butter to a bubble. Add leeks. Reduce heat and simmer for 5 minutes, stirring with a wooden spoon. Add white wine, honey, white pepper and tarragon leaves and continue to simmer for 15 minutes. Leeks should be soft and wine evaporated. Place sour cream in a mixing bowl. Slowly add leek mixture to sour cream, stirring to incorporate.

Add half the caviar and fold in gently. Place sauce on top of fish and garnish with a small dollop of caviar.

Honey Mustard Sauce

1/2 celery, peeled and diced
1/2 c. carrots, peeled and diced
1/2 c. red onion, diced
1 T. olive oil
2 cloves garlic, minced
1 T. flour
2 tsp. lemon juice

1 c. chicken stock
(see recipe p. 47)
1 c. honey
1 T. honey
1 T. fresh tarragon
1/2 c. tomatoes, cut into
1/4-inch cubes

Peel celery and carrots with a potato peeler. Dice celery carrots and onion into 1/4-inch cubes (the smaller the better).

Heat sauté pan to hot. When oil is hot, add garlic, celery, carrots and onion and sauté until vegetables are tender. Do not brown. Sprinkle flour over vegetables and gently combine with a wooden spoon. Add lemon juice and chicken stock. Bring to a boil. Simmer on low heat for 5 minutes. Gently add mustard, honey, tarragon and chopped tomatoes. Simmer 2 minutes.

Combine well. Keep warm.

CHEF'S TIPS

• If honey mustard is not available, use 1 cup Dijon mustard with 2 tablespoons honey.

Thousand Island Dressing

1 c. sour cream
2 c. mayonnaise
2 eggs, hard-cooked and diced into 1/4-inch pieces
3/4 c. chili sauce
1/4 c. ketchup
1/2 c. red peppers, diced into 1/4-inch pieces

1 1/2 T. chopped parsley, leaves only
1 tsp. lemon juice
1 tsp. Worcestershire sauce
1/2 tsp. black pepper
1 tsp. salt

Combine all ingredients and mix together gently and thoroughly. Keep refrigerated in a covered container up to 30 days.

Makes 1 quart.

CHEF'S TIPS

• To make Russian dressing add 1/2 cup black caviar. Fold in gently.
• To make sauce Rémoulade, add 1 tablespoon capers and 10 anchovies minced fine.

CHEF'S TIPS

- For smooth and lump-free sauce, put cooked sauce in a blender on medium speed for 1 minute, or pour through a fine strainer.
- Do not use a stainless steel pot. It scorches too easily.

CHEF'S TIPS

- This is a very tasty sauce with all kinds of fish.
- To make this sauce on the lighter side, use low-fat mayonnaise and cottage cheese.

Basic White or Cream Sauce

Light Version:
1 qt. milk or half-and-half
3 oz. roux (see recipe p. 180)

Medium Version:
1 qt. milk or half-and-half
4 oz. roux

Heavy Version:
1 qt. milk or half-and-half
6 oz. roux

In a heavy saucepot, heat liquid to a simmer. With a wire whisk, add roux and whisk smooth. Avoid touching sides or bottom of pan while whisking. Simmer on low heat for 15 minutes, stirring often with a wooden spoon.

To keep mixture from sticking to the sides and bottom of the pan, stir with a rubber spatula.

Makes approximately 1 quart.

Cucumber Sauce

8 oz. cottage cheese
1 tsp. lemon juice
$\frac{1}{2}$ tsp. lime juice
pinch white pepper
$\frac{1}{4}$ tsp. salt

$\frac{1}{4}$ tsp. Worcestershire sauce
$\frac{1}{2}$ c. mayonnaise
$\frac{1}{4}$ tsp. tarragon leaves
$\frac{2}{3}$ c. cucumbers, peeled and shredded

In a blender container, place cottage cheese, lemon juice, lime juice, white pepper, salt, Worcestershire sauce, mayonnaise and tarragon. Blend smooth. Place in a bowl.

Peel and shred cucumbers. Add to cottage cheese puree and combine well. Chill and serve.

Makes 1 pint.

John's Blender Hollandaise

2 whole eggs and 1 egg yolk (or ¾ cup ultra-pasteurized homogenized eggs)
2 tsp. chicken base
2 tsp. lemon juice
4 drops Tabasco sauce
1 pt. clarified butter (see recipe p. 189)

Put eggs, chicken base, lemon juice and Tabasco sauce in a blender container. Mix for 5 seconds on low speed. Place a piece of aluminum foil over the top of the container and form a pocket in the foil. Make a small 1/16-inch-diameter hole in the bottom of the pocket. This is to make an even, steady stream so that clarified butter and egg mixture can form an emulsion. Heat clarified butter to exactly 140°. Use a food thermometer to measure temperature exactly.

Turn blender to medium speed and add butter as needed to base. Sauce should be lemon-colored and thick. You may not need all the warm butter.

- Butter is heated to 140° to help form the emulsion. If butter is too hot, it will cook the eggs. If butter is too cold, it will not combine with the eggs. The temperature must be exactly at 140°. You cannot guess or approximate the temperature.

- To make sauce mousseline, combine 1 cup hollandaise sauce and 1 cup unsweetened whipped cream in a stainless steel bowl and gently fold with a wire whisk to make a light, lemony sauce. Use sauce mousseline as a glaze topping on fish, after broiling it to a golden brown under a broiler.

CHEF'S TIPS

- This recipe is easy to master and consistently makes excellent hollandaise sauce.
- Use level teaspoons in this recipe.
- Take care that the small hole in the bottom of the foil pocket does not exceed 1/16 inch.
- Pasteurized, homogenized eggs greatly reduce the risk of food-borne illness.

ANGLING TIP

Choose live bait for walleye fishing according to season: During summer, use leeches or night crawlers. In the fall, large minnows get the most action.

BASES

Roux

1 lb. margarine
1 lb. flour

Preheat oven to 350°

In a heavy 2-quart saucepot or baking dish, melt margarine. Stir in flour and bake for 1 hour at 350°. Stir the mixture every 20 minutes. When cooked, the roux should be golden brown and the consistency of wheat sand.

It is always better to use roux at room temperature. Roux keeps well in the refrigerator or freezer.

- Sauces and gravies are among the most important components of great cooking. Roux thickens sauces and gravies. Although roux is only one of many cooking thickeners, I have concluded after 35 years of professional cooking that it is the best thickener.

- It is very important to weigh the flour for this recipe and not measure it.

CHEF'S TIPS

• Pour roux into ice cube trays and freeze. When frozen, place in resealable plastic bags. Thaw 10 to 15 minutes before using.

Mushroom Flour Meal and Variations

3 lbs. fresh crimini or button mushrooms
1 tsp. salt (the finer the better)

Preheat oven to 180°.

Toss vegetables with salt. Place on a wire rack over a baking pan. Place in a 180° oven for 12 to 14 hours. When vegetables are totally dry, break into small pieces and make into flour meal using either a food processor or blender. Be careful not to overgrind. Keep in tightly covered glass jar.

To make other kinds of vegetable meal:

For carrot flour meal, substitute 3 lbs. carrots, peeled and sliced into 1/4-inch strips for mushrooms

For zucchini flour meal, substitute 3 lbs. zucchini

For summer squash flour meal, substitute 3 lbs. summer squash

For horseradish flour meal, substitute 3 lbs. horseradish

CHEF'S TIPS

• I use a food processor or blender to make this meal. If you have neither, place dry pieces in a double-thick plastic bag and gently mash with a meat mallet or saucepot.
• Try to keep meal the size of cornmeal. A few large pieces are better than all dust.

Fresh Bread Crumbs

1 lb. loaf white bread

Remove crust from bottom. Cut slices in half. Place in a food processor and make into medium to fine crumbs. A blender also works well. Add 4 half-slices, one at a time. Blend on medium speed to make crumbs. Remove crumbs to a bowl. Repeat until all crumbs are made.

For different flavors: use whole wheat bread, light rye bread or pumpernickel bread.

- Making fresh bread crumbs is an important and often overlooked detail of cooking. Fresh bread crumbs are far superior to prepared crumbs which become overcooked, dry and tasteless.

- Only make as many crumbs as you need.

Seasoned Flour

1 c. all-purpose flour
2 tsp. salt
1/8 tsp. white pepper

Combine well.

The reason for using white pepper is so that the flour does not appear to have black flecks.

Never reuse excess flour.

Makes 1 cup.

Egg Wash

2 eggs
1/4 c. milk

Break eggs into a bowl. Add milk. Whisk to a froth.

Never keep egg wash after use. It is a medium for bacteria. If you need a small amount, make half a batch.

Makes ¾ cup.

CHEF'S TIPS

- Do not use leftover crumbs. You run the risk of food poisoning.
- If crumbs are refrigerated too long, they will mold.

ANGLING TIP

If you keep losing your plastic worm in heavy weeds, put a dab of crazy glue on the hook before sliding on the worm.

SEASONINGS

Sachet Bag

cheesecloth or tea ball
1 T. chopped parsley with stems
1 tsp. fresh thyme
2 bay leaves
½ tsp. black peppercorns
3 cloves garlic, crushed
4 whole cloves

    To make sachet bag, cut cheesecloth into an 8-inch square. Place spices in center. Gather corners together and tie a string near the top, leaving room for the liquid to circulate through the spices. Cut off extra cheesecloth on top of the bag.

- The reason for the bag is to be able to remove spices from the liquid. You could also use a large tea ball but the cheesecloth works better.

- The purpose of a sachet bag is to produce a balance of seasoning for stocks and soups, while being able to remove all the spice ingredients when desired.

ANGLING TIP

When using soft lures (like rubber worms) to fish for bass, most bites will occur as your lure falls to the bottom. If a fish doesn't bite as the lure drops, try a lift-and-drop retrieve, just like jig-fishing for walleye.

Chef John's Fish Rub

1/2 tsp. garlic powder
1/2 tsp. freshly ground black pepper
1 tsp. dry thyme
1 T. dry tarragon
1/2 tsp. Hungarian paprika
1 tsp. onion powder
1/4 tsp. ground allspice
1/4 tsp. dry mustard

Combine all ingredients and keep in a tightly sealed container. Rub on fish fillets or fish steaks and place in a sealable plastic bag with 2 tablespoons vegetable oil for at least 2 hours to fuse the flavors. Grill or sauté.

• There is no salt in this recipe as salt draws out the moisture from the fish. Salt should only be added after cooking.

Makes 2½ T.

CHEF'S TIPS
• The rub will not tenderize fish.
• Please add any spices or herbs you like.

Pickling Spice Bag

3 T. pickling spice
8-inch square cheesecloth
butcher string

To make spice bag, cut cheesecloth into an 8-inch square. Place spices in center. Gather corners together and tie a string near the top, leaving room for the liquid to circulate through the spices. Cut off extra cheesecloth on top of the bag.

CHEF'S TIPS
• The reason for the bag is to be able to remove spices from the liquid. You could also use a large tea ball but the cheesecloth works better.

CHEF'S TIPS

• Szechuan pepper-corns come from a prickly ash tree. They impart a mildly-hot spice flavor and are worth the search.

Five-Spice Powder

1 tsp. ground anise
1 1/2 tsp. ground fennel seeds
1 tsp. ground Szechuan or white peppercorns
1/2 tsp. ground cinnamon
1/2 tsp. ground cloves

To grind spices, use a spice or electric coffee grinder. Do not grind too finely. Keep in tightly covered container.

Makes 4½ tablespoons.

Spiced Salt

1 tsp. cumin seeds
1 tsp. fennel seeds
1 tsp. Szechuan peppercorns
1/2 tsp. white peppercorns
4 whole cloves
1/2 tsp. celery seeds
1 tsp. seeds from a green bell pepper
1/2 c. kosher salt

In a nonstick skillet, place all seeds and berries. Heat to medium. Stir seeds slowly with a wooden spoon for about 3 minutes until aromatic. Remove to a plate and let cool. Grind in a spice grinder. Mix with kosher salt. Keep in a covered glass jar.

Use this as a dip or serve with fried foods.

Makes ½ cup.

ANGLING TIP

Fish for crappie around vegetation and other structure such as stumps, brush and logs.

Curry Powder

¼ c. coriander seeds
2 T. cumin seeds
1 T. 3-pepper-blend peppercorns
2 cinnamon sticks, crushed
1 T. ground turmeric
2 tsp. whole cardamom seeds
1 tsp. whole cloves
1 tsp. whole allspice seeds
2 tsp. fennel seeds
1 tsp. brown mustard seeds
1 tsp. dried chili pepper, stemmed and seeded
1 tsp. ground ginger

Place all ingredients, except ground ginger, in a metal baking pan. Roast at 300° for 7 minutes. (Not one minute longer, or it will make spices bitter.) Transfer to a plate. Let spices cool. When spices have cooled, grind spices to a fine powder in a spice or coffee grinder. Combine with ground ginger. Store in a sealed glass jar away from heat and light.

Dried chili pepper choices on a hotness scale of 1 (mild) to 10 (very hot):
- Guajillo, heat 2 to 4
- Ancho, heat 3 to 5
- Habanero, heat 10

Makes ½ cup.

CHEF'S TIPS

• If you want mild curry powder, leave out the chili peppers.

DRESSINGS

CHEF'S TIPS

• If you are a purist, use pine nuts instead of almond slices.

Almond Pesto

²/₃ c. extra virgin olive oil
¹/₂ c. unsalted almonds, roasted
¹/₄ tsp. salt
2 cloves garlic, minced fine
¹/₄ tsp. lime zest
freshly ground 3-pepper blend to taste
2 c. fresh basil leaves
¹/₄ c. Parmesan cheese, freshly grated

To roast almonds, roll almonds in 2 teaspoons olive oil and roast in a 350° oven for 10 minutes. Let cool.

In a blender cup, place ²/₃ cup olive oil, roasted almonds, salt, garlic, lime zest and pepper and puree on low speed for 30 seconds. Add chopped basil leaves and puree until basil leaves are small flakes. Add Parmesan cheese and puree to combine. Remove and keep in a covered glass container in refrigerator until needed.

Makes 1 cup.

ANGLING TIP

When fishing for salmon moving upstream in the fall, use spawn sacs, yarn flies and streamer flies.

Flavored Mayonnaise

Base

  1 c. mayonnaise
  $\frac{1}{8}$ tsp. white pepper
  $\frac{1}{4}$ tsp. salt
  $\frac{1}{2}$ tsp. lemon juice
  $\frac{1}{2}$ tsp. Worcestershire sauce
  1$\frac{1}{2}$ tsp. sugar

In a bowl, whisk all ingredients smooth. Place in a covered glass container in refrigerator until service.

- Do not make too much mayonnaise at one time.
- If adding a seasoning with salt, leave the salt out of the base.

For variations, add one or a combination of the following ingredients to the base:

  1 tsp. curry powder
  1 tsp. Cajun spice mix
  1 tsp. taco mix
  1 T. fresh herbs, chopped fine
  1 tsp. lemon pepper
  1 T. currant jelly
  1 T. hot pepper jelly
  1 roasted red pepper (seeds and skin removed)
  1 T. fresh blue cheese

CHEF'S TIPS

• The purpose of heating the oil and pouring it through a small hole is to create an emulsion. This will keep the salad dressing from separating.

Easy Caesar Dressing

¾ c. red wine vinegar
4 oz. anchovy fillets in oil
1 T. yellow mustard
2 T. Worcestershire sauce
1 T. black pepper
2 cloves garlic, minced fine
2 tsp. lemon juice
1 tsp. chicken base
4 drops Tabasco sauce
3 c. olive oil
½ c. Parmesan cheese, shredded

In a blender, add all ingredients except olive oil and Parmesan cheese. Heat oil to 140°. Check temperature with a food thermometer.

Place a piece of foil on top of the blender and make a deep pocket. Punch a small hole (¹⁄₁₆-inch diameter) in the bottom of the pocket. Turn blender on high speed. Pour warm oil into the foil pocket. The dressing will thicken. Place in a storage container. Add Parmesan cheese and combine well.

Makes 1 quart.

CHEF'S TIPS

• The hardest thing about pineapple mayonnaise is not drinking it like a milk shake.

Pineapple Mayonnaise

1½ c. mayonnaise
½ tsp. Worcestershire sauce
2 tsp. sugar
½ tsp. lemon juice
⅔ c. pineapple tidbits, drained
1 T. fresh tarragon

Place all ingredients in a blender container and blend until smooth. Store covered in a glass container. Keeps 1 week.

Makes 2 cups.

BUTTERS

Citrus Butters

Lemon Butter:

1 lb. butter
1/4 c. shallots, minced fine
1 T. lemon juice
4 drops Tabasco sauce

pinch white pepper
1/2 tsp. lemon zest, grated
2 T. fresh chives, cut into
1/4-inch pieces

In a small skillet, heat 1 tablespoon butter to a fast bubble. Add shallots and sauté until tender. Add juice and simmer for 1 minute. Pour into a medium mixing bowl. Add Tabasco, white pepper and zest. Add chives and remaining butter at room temperature. Mix well to combine.

Roll into a 1-inch-diameter log and cover with a plastic wrap. Chill or freeze. For service, cut a generous piece and top fish or serve with roll or biscuits.

Variations:

Lime Butter - substitute lime juice and zest for lemon juice and zest

Orange Butter - substitute orange juice and zest for lemon juice and zest

Tangerine Butter - substitute tangerine juice and zest for lemon juice and zest

Grapefruit Butter - substitute grapefruit juice and zest for lemon juice and zest

Clarified Butter

1 lb. butter

This is sometimes known as "drawn butter." Place butter in a saucepan at low heat until it is completely melted. Remove all foam which rises to the top of liquid. Take from heat and let stand until all milk solids have fallen to the bottom of the pot. With a ladle, remove all clear oil and keep.

Makes 1 1/2 cups (12 oz.).

CHEF'S TIPS

• It is important to remove all white membrane from the zest of citrus fruits; this membrane is very bitter.

CHEF'S TIPS

• I prefer to use half margarine and butter. The margarine will increase the smoke-point temperature, allowing the liquid to be heated to a higher temperature without burning.

Anchovy-Caper Butter

½ lb. salted butter, softened
¼ c. shallots, minced
2 T. anchovies, mashed to a puree

¼ tsp. freshly ground white pepper
1 tsp. Worcestershire sauce
1½ T. capers, drained

Melt 1 tablespoon butter in a small pan. Add shallots and sauté until clear and tender. Remove from heat. Add anchovy puree, white pepper, Worcestershire sauce and capers and combine well. Place in a medium bowl. Add remaining butter and combine well. Lay a 12-inch-long sheet of plastic wrap on a flat surface. Place butter mixture 2 inches from the top in a rope shape. Roll into a log and chill or freeze until needed.

CHEF'S TIPS

- Ghee is a recipe from India. It is one step better than clarified butter.
- I keep the bottom milk solids in a separate glass jar and add it to vegetables or mashed potatoes for flavor.
- Ghee will become very salty if you use salted butter.

Ghee

3 lbs. unsalted butter

In a heavy 3- to 4-quart saucepan, heat butter on low heat until melted. Increase heat and bring liquid butter to a boil. Reduce heat to a simmer. Simmer uncovered and undisturbed until the bottom milk solids have turned from white to golden brown. A thin crust will form on top. Remove crust with a skimmer. Very carefully remove pot from stove. Let cool for 15 to 20 minutes. Without disturbing the bottom, ladle off the liquid oil or ghee. Pour through a dish towel-lined sieve. Stop before disturbing bottom solids. Keeps in a glass jar covered tightly in refrigerator up to 3 months.

Variations

For curry flavor - combine 1/2 cup ghee, 1/2 teaspoon curry powder (see recipe p. 158) and 1/2 teaspoon lemon zest. Pour into ice cube trays, filling each compartment halfway. Place in refrigerator to harden. Just before service, remove ghee from ice cube trays by setting at room temperature for a few minutes

For Cumin flavor - add 3 tablespoons cumin seeds in a cheesecloth bag to melted butter

For Peppercorn flavor - add 2 tablespoons black, white or green peppercorns in a cheesecloth bag to melted butter

For Ginger flavor - add a 2-inch piece ginger, peeled and diced into 8 pieces, in a cheesecloth bag to melted butter

For Spiced flavor - add 25 whole cloves, 2 tablespoons sesame seeds, 1 tablespoon whole allspice and 1 stick cinnamon, cut in half, in a cheesecloth bag to melted butter

Green Peppercorn-Lemon-Caper Butter

2 tsp. lemon zest
1 T. lemon juice
1 lb. butter, room temperature (salted)
1 T. capers, drained
1 1/2 tsp. green peppercorns, drained
3 drops Tabasco sauce

Remove zest from a lemon with a potato peeler and mince fine. Squeeze juice from lemon.

Place butter in a mixing bowl. Add all ingredients and combine well.

Make logs by placing a sheet of waxed paper, one foot long, on a flat surface. Place butter on waxed paper 3 inches from the bottom. Form into a log. Roll waxed paper into a cylinder. Freeze in a sealable plastic bag. To serve, cut from logs as needed.

CHEF'S TIPS

• It is all right to use all capers or all green peppercorns. The capers give a zesty vinegar flavor. The green peppercorns give a medium-hot pepper flavor.

Stilton Shallot Butter

1 1/2 c. butter
1/4 c. shallots, diced into
1/4-inch pieces
1/2 tsp. garlic powder
1/2 c. Stilton cheese, crumbled

1/2 tsp. lemon zest, grated
3 drops Tabasco sauce
1 pinch white pepper
1 tsp. fresh tarragon, chopped

Heat 1/4 cup butter in a small saucepan. Add shallots and cook until tender. Remove to a bowl. Refrigerate to chill. Add all ingredients to the bowl. With a large spoon, combine well. Butter should be the consistency of thick mayonnaise. Spoon onto a sheet of plastic wrap. Roll up into 2 logs and chill. Cut off desired amount when ready to use.

CHEF'S TIPS

• This can be frozen and used from a frozen state.
• You may substitute blue cheese or Gorgonzola cheese for Stilton cheese; however, Stilton cheese has the richest flavor.

- You can also use this batter with crayfish or crab.

Shrimp Butter

1 lb. butter
1 c. shallots, diced into ¼-inch pieces
1 clove garlic, minced fine
1 lb. shrimp, unpeeled
1 roasted red pepper, skinned, seeded (see recipe p. 195)
1 T. lemon juice
½ tsp. lemon zest, grated
1 tsp. Worcestershire sauce
¼ c. golden sherry

Heat butter on medium heat in a heavy saucepan until hot. Do not brown. Add shallots, garlic and shrimp. Simmer for 5 minutes. Remove shrimp to cool and add red pepper, lemon juice, zest, Worcestershire sauce and sherry. Simmer just below a boil for 20 minutes, uncovered. Peel and remove the veins from shrimp. Cut each cooked shrimp into 4 pieces.

After 20 minutes, place butter base in a blender cup. Add shrimp. Cover and blend on medium speed until shrimp are pureed smooth. Pour into a large shallow bowl. Refrigerate until butter sets but before it becomes hardened. Stir to combine. Place a sheet of plastic wrap on a flat surface. Top with butter. Roll into a 1-inch-diameter log. Refrigerate or freeze. When ready to use, cut into 1-inch slices.

OTHERS

Ruby Red Grapefruit and Lemon- Mango Compote

1/4 c. fresh orange juice
1/3 c. brown sugar
2 ruby red grapefruit, peeled and segmented
2 tsp. fresh ginger, minced fine
1/8 tsp. salt
1/2 tsp. ground cinnamon
1 T. cornstarch
2 T. fresh orange juice
1/4 c. maple syrup
2 ripe mangos, diced into 1/2-inch cubes

To segment grapefruit: With a sharp fillet knife, remove skin. Slice each section alongside each membrane wall and remove wedge. Strain over a bowl to collect the juice. Squeeze juice out of grapefruit core.

In a small saucepan, heat orange juice, brown sugar and juice from segmenting the grapefruit.

Let simmer for 3 minutes. Add ginger and salt. Combine cinnamon, cornstarch, orange juice and maple syrup into a smooth paste. Add to sauce and simmer until sauce is thick, clear and shiny. Stir often with a wooden spoon. Add mango and grapefruit to sauce very gently and simmer for 10 minutes. Combine very gently. Let cool.

Cover and refrigerate.

Pineapple Pear Confiture

4 c. fresh pineapple chunks
4 ripe pears, peeled, cored, cut into 1/4-inch cubes
1/3 c. fresh lemon juice
2 c. brown sugar
2 c. powdered sugar
1/2 tsp. ground nutmeg
1/2 tsp. ground cinnamon
1 T. fresh tarragon

In a heavy saucepan, combine fruit and lemon juice. Bring to a brisk boil. Combine sugars and spices. Add to fruit. Reduce to low heat. Stir to combine. Let simmer for 1 1/2 hours, stirring often. When mixture drips thick from a spoon, remove and place in a glass container to cool.

Refrigerate until needed.

CHEF'S TIPS

• All types of grapefruit can be used in this recipe.

CHEF'S TIPS

• For extra zip, add a chili pepper with the seeds and stem removed.

CHEF'S TIPS

• For a variation, add ½ cup golden raisins and 1 tablespoon minced fresh ginger to this recipe.

Pineapple Salsa

4 c. fresh ripe tomatoes
2 jalapeño peppers, seeded and diced into ¼-inch pieces
1 c. red onion, diced into ¼-inch pieces
1 c. red pepper, diced into ¼-inch pieces
1 c. green onion, sliced ¼ inch thick
¼ c. olive oil
1 T. Worcestershire sauce
1½ T. molasses
2 tsp. celery salt
½ tsp. black pepper
½ tsp. ground ginger
¼ tsp. ground cinnamon
2 T. brown sugar
2 c. fresh pineapple, diced into ½-inch pieces
2 T. cilantro, chopped

Remove stem end from fully ripened tomatoes. Dice tomatoes, jalapeño peppers, red onion, red pepper into ¼-inch cubes. Heat olive oil hot in a skillet. Add red onion, red pepper and green onions and sauté for 2 minutes. Add Worcestershire sauce, molasses, celery salt, black pepper, ground ginger, cinnamon and brown sugar. Bring to a rolling boil. Remove from heat. Add jalapeño peppers, pineapple, cilantro and tomatoes. Place in a bowl and refrigerate until cool.

Store in a covered glass container.

CHEF'S TIPS

• Keep this relish covered in refrigerator up to 2 months.

• One-fourth cup Grand Marnier makes a nice addition to this recipe.

Cranraisin Relish

2 oranges, chopped fine
1 lb. dried cranberries
½ c. orange juice concentrate
2 c. water
2 T. balsamic vinegar
1 c. sugar
2 T. cornstarch

Wash and remove stems from oranges. Cut into ½-inch slices and remove the seeds. Grind or chop slices into fine pieces. Set aside.

Place cranberries, orange juice concentrate, water and balsamic vinegar in a pan. Simmer for 20 minutes. Combine the sugar and cornstarch. Add to pan with oranges, stirring well. Simmer for 20 minutes over low heat, stirring often to keep from burning.

Roasted Red Pepper Coulis

5 large roasted red peppers (see below)
2 T. olive oil
2 cloves garlic, minced
1/2 c. shallots, chopped
1 T. Worcestershire sauce
1/4 tsp. black pepper
1 tsp. salt
1/3 c. dry red wine
1 T. dill pickle juice
2 T. fresh cilantro leaves
2 tsp. brown sugar

Roast peppers. Remove skin, stem and seeds. Dice into large pieces.

Heat oven to 375°.

Heat oil on medium heat in a heavy sauté pan. Add garlic and shallots. Sauté until shallots are soft and clear. Add peppers. Cover and bake in a 375° oven for 30 minutes. Remove. Add remaining ingredients and bring to a boil. Place in a blender and puree until smooth. Remove and strain through a fine strainer. Keep refrigerated in covered container.

Makes 1 pint.

How to Roast Peppers

Place peppers on a burner over an open flame or under a broiler and roast until skins blacken. Turn and repeat on all sides. Remove and place in a paper bag. Close tightly and let sit for 15 minutes. Remove peppers and brush off skins. Pull off stems and clean out seeds. If using hot peppers, wear rubber gloves.

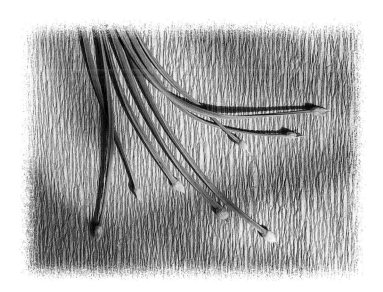

CHEF'S TIPS

• If shallots are not available, use red onions.

ANGLING TIP

When choosing lures, remember that fish use hearing, smell and sight to locate food. For predator fish, hearing is most important.

Three Colors of Pepper Coulis

1 1/2 T. olive oil
1 c. red onion, diced
3 cloves garlic, whole
1/2 tsp. salt
1/4 tsp. white pepper
1 c. heavy cream
2 large roasted red peppers (see recipe p. 195)
2 large roasted green peppers
2 large roasted yellow peppers

In a skillet, heat oil. Add onions and garlic and sauté until soft. Place onions, garlic, salt and pepper in a blender cup and puree smooth. Place puree in a bowl. Combine with cream. To make three colors of pepper coulis, place 1/3 base with each color roasted pepper in a blender cup (do one at a time). Puree and put individual colored coulis in separate squeeze-bottle containers.

To serve, paint plates with each color pepper coulis or put 1 teaspoon of each color on the edge of the plate.

CHEF'S TIPS

• If you are truly a hot, hot pepper fanat-ic, add one seeded, diced habanero pepper. Remove all the white membranes and use rubber gloves. (That's a hint to let you know how hot habaneros are.)

Peach and Black Cherry Chutney

1 T. olive oil
1/4 c. red onion, diced into 1/4-inch pieces
2 cloves garlic, minced fine
2 T. balsamic vinegar
1 T. honey
2 tsp. fresh gingerroot, minced fine
1/2 c. golden raisins
2 c. frozen peach slices, cut into 1/2-inch cubes
2 c. frozen black cherries and liquid
2 roasted poblano peppers, peeled, diced into 1/4-inch pieces (see recipe, opposite)
1 1/2 T. brown sugar
1/2 tsp. ground cloves
1 tsp. ground nutmeg
1/2 tsp. ground cinnamon
1 T. cornstarch
1/4 tsp. black pepper
1/4 c. orange juice

Heat oil until hot in a saucepan. Add onion and garlic and sauté until onion is tender. Add vinegar, honey, ginger and raisins and bring to a boil. Add peaches, black cherries and poblano peppers and return to a boil. Reduce heat and simmer for 10 minutes, stirring often to keep mixture from sticking. Combine brown sugar, cloves, nutmeg, cinnamon and cornstarch. Add to base. Stir in well. Add black pepper and orange juice. Cook until sauce is clear and shiny. Remove to a bowl and cool. Keep refrigerated until service.

CHEF'S TIPS

• For a variation, add a
red or green pepper.

Roasted Tomato Coulis

12 plum tomatoes, stems removed, chopped coarsely
1 c. red onions, cut into ¼-inch slices
3 cloves garlic, cut into ¼-inch cubes
1 T. fresh thyme leaves
2 T. olive oil
¼ tsp. black pepper
½ tsp. salt
½ c. dry red wine
1½ T. flour

Preheat oven to 350°.

Remove stem and cut tomatoes into 8 pieces. Remove stem core from red onion and slice into thin slices. Dice garlic and chop fresh thyme. In a large bowl, place all ingredients except tomatoes and flour. Combine well. In shallow baking pan, roast tomatoes in a 350° oven for 1 hour. Stir from time to time. Remove pan from oven and sift flour over tomatoes. Return to oven and bake for 30 minutes. Remove from oven. Place all ingredients in a blender. Puree on medium for 2 minutes. Pour through a coarse strainer. Shake strainer from side to side to let liquid through. Toss seeds and skins. Return puree to blender and puree smooth on high speed.

Place in a covered glass container in the refrigerator until needed. Serve with cold or hot fish.

Makes 2 pints.

ANGLING TIP

The best method
for catching Chinook
salmon in deep lakes
is trolling with a plug or
spoon. Use downriggers
to get the lure down
to where the fish are
swimming.

CHEF'S TIPS

• This recipe comes from Malaysia and Southern India.

• This is a paste of hot chili peppers, spices and lemon juice. I added fruits for this interpretation.

Fruited Chili Sambal

2 T. peanut oil
1/2 c. red onion, diced into 1/4-inch pieces
2 cloves garlic, minced fine
1/4 c. hot green or red chili peppers, diced into 1/4-inch cubes, stems and seeds removed
2 tsp. fresh ginger, minced fine
1/4 c. molasses
1 T. brown sugar
1/8 tsp. ground nutmeg
2 T. balsamic vinegar
2 T. fish sauce (optional)
1 c. crushed pineapple
2 ripe peaches, peeled, pitted and diced into 1/4-inch cubes
1 tsp. lemon zest, grated
1/4 tsp. salt
1/8 tsp. black pepper

In a medium-sized skillet, heat peanut oil to hot. Add onion and garlic and sauté until onions are tender, not brown. Add chili peppers and ginger. Sauté 2 minutes. Add molasses, brown sugar, nutmeg, balsamic vinegar and fish sauce. Bring to a boil. Add pineapple, peaches, lemon zest, salt and pepper. Simmer on low for 15 minutes.

CHEF'S TIPS

• This confiture can be made in advance and reheated. Keep in a covered glass container in the refrigerator until needed. When confiture is cooked, it will be the consistency of jam.

Red Onion Confiture

1/4 c. clarified butter (see recipe p. 189)
6 c. red onion, cut into 1/4-inch slices
1/2 c. dry sherry
2 T. balsamic vinegar
2 T. brown sugar
1/4 c. honey

In a heavy saucepot, heat butter. Add onions and sauté until clear and tender, stirring often with a wooden spoon. Reduce heat. Simmer for 15 minutes. Add sherry and balsamic vinegar and simmer 20 minutes more, stirring often. Add brown sugar and honey. Simmer an additional 20 minutes. Place in a bowl for service.

Makes 1 pint.

NOTES

FISHIN' AND FARMIN'

My dad was a Scandinavian-American Minnesota farmer, as were all of his relatives and friends. They fished whenever possible, but only after morning chores were done and before evening chores started. Milking cows twice a day took precedence over everything.

Our fishing trips were often successful. My job was to clean the fish on the old wooden ironing board in the milk house and take them to my mother so we could enjoy them for supper. Mom had rules: You catch it, you clean it, I'll cook it. No exceptions. It was well worth it, as she is still holds the title of best cook in the family.

Dad and I would finish up chores, close the barn doors and head toward the house. It was exactly 100 feet from the barn to the farmhouse. Halfway there I would raise my nose like a young bull elk, take in a deep breath and tell my father what was on the menu for dinner in great detail: fried panfish, fresh corn on the cob, hash brown potatoes with heavy cream, shredded garden onions with a hint of nutmeg, home-made Parker House Rolls, iceberg lettuce with red dressings and hot Devil's Food cake with chocolate brick frosting and vanilla ice cream from the Schwan's man.

My predictions were accurate 99% of the time, much to the amazement of my father.

I am forever grateful to my parents; my work ethic, love of fishing and cooking began in this nightly ritual.

Side Dishes

Potatoes

CHEF'S TIPS

• For fun variations:
Add 1/2 cup diced
onion, 1/2 cup
cooked bacon
pieces and/or 1
teaspoon fresh
dill weed.

Rösti Potatoes

1 1/2 lbs. potatoes
8 oz. Swiss cheese
1 tsp. salt
1/8 tsp. white pepper

Boil potatoes until tender and drain immediately. Cool well and peel. Shred into a bowl. Shred Swiss cheese into same bowl. Add salt and pepper and mix well. Fry in a hot, buttered cast iron skillet or nonstick pan. Brown on one side and turn. Serve directly from skillet to table.

Serves 4.

Herb and Cheese Baked Sweet Potato Fans

4 medium, evenly-sized sweet potatoes
3 T. soft butter
1 T. fresh tarragon, chopped medium
2 tsp. fresh thyme, chopped medium
1/3 c. Parmesan cheese, grated
1/3 c. chicken stock (see recipe p. 47)
1/3 c. cheddar cheese, grated

Preheat oven to 350°.

Peel 2/3 of each potato. Leave a strip on the bottom. Cut potato crosswise into 1/8-inch slices, leaving 1/4 inch on bottom to hold potato together. Place potatoes in a baking dish and run cold water over each one to help fan out slightly. Drain well. Combine butter, herbs and Parmesan cheese together. Spread paste over potatoes evenly. Add chicken stock. Cover and bake for 40 minutes. Uncover and top potatoes with Cheddar cheese. Bake, uncovered, for 20 minutes more. When potatoes are tender, serve with fish.

Serves 4.

CHEF'S TIPS

• You can use white
baking potatoes in
this recipe.

• Peel and cut carrots
in half and place
in between the
potatoes.

• Grated fresh
Parmesan is best.

• *For slicing potatoes, place a wooden pencil on each side of the potato and slice thin potato slices holding knife level. Pencils will keep you from slicing all the way through.*

Grandma Schumacher's Hash Browns

6 c. grated raw potatoes
2 tsp. fresh lemon juice
1/2 cup onion, diced into 1/4-inch pieces
1/2 c. heavy cream
1 T. fresh tarragon or cilantro
1 tsp. salt
1/4 tsp. white pepper
1/4 c. butter

Grate or shred potatoes. Put potatoes and lemon juice in a bowl and let sit for 10 minutes. Drain off excess liquids. Add onions, cream, tarragon, salt and pepper. Mix.

In a medium, nonstick frying pan, bring butter to a fast bubble. Add potato batter and cover. Cook on medium heat until potatoes are golden brown. Turn potatoes, cover and steam through. Potatoes should be golden brown on both sides. Remove from pan and cut into squares.

Serves 4.

CHEF'S TIPS

• Be careful not to use too large a frying pan. Potato squares should be about 2 inches thick. If you're using an electric frying pan, cut the potato cake into quarters before turning.

Great Mashed Potatoes and Variations

4 to 6 russet potatoes, peeled or unpeeled (your choice)
1 T. salt in enough cold water to cover potatoes
1/2 c. butter
1/4 c. heavy cream
1 tsp. salt
1/4 tsp. freshly ground white pepper

Wash potatoes well. Cut into quarters. Place in a large pot. Cover with cold water and add 1 tablespoon salt. Boil at a slow roll until potatoes are tender when poked with a thin paring knife. Drain off all water. Let potatoes steam off for 4 to 5 minutes. Add butter, cream, salt and pepper. Mash until creamy.

Mashed Potato Variations

Roasted Garlic Mashed Potatoes
1/3 c. peeled whole garlic cloves
1/2 c. butter

Place garlic cloves and butter in a small covered saucepot. The smaller the saucepot, the better. Roast in a 325° oven for 1 hour. Remove from oven. Place garlic and liquid in blender and puree. If more liquid is needed to puree, add cream. Add garlic puree mixture to potatoes while mashing. The garlic puree can be made in advance and kept in a covered glass jar in the refrigerator.

Roasted Poblano Pepper and Cilantro Mashed Potatoes
1 roasted poblano pepper, seeds and stem removed
(see recipe on roasting peppers p. 193)
1/2 c. butter
1/3 c. peeled whole garlic cloves
1 T. fresh cilantro, minced fine

Remove stem and seeds from pepper. Place in a small covered saucepot with butter and garlic. Bake at 325° for 1 hour. Remove and puree to a fine consistency. Add to potatoes while mashing. When finished mashing, fold in cilantro.

Country Mashed Potatoes
1 1/2 c. sour cream
1/3 c. cooked bacon pieces
1/3 c. green onions, sliced thin
1/8 tsp. black pepper

After potatoes are steamed off, add sour cream. Mash. Fold in bacon, green onions and black pepper.

Celery Mashed Potatoes
1/2 c. butter
2 c. celery, peeled and sliced into 1/2-inch pieces

Place the butter and celery in a covered saucepot and bake at 325° for 30 minutes. Mash with potatoes. The most important thing with this variation is to peel all strings off celery with a potato peeler before baking.

CHEF'S TIPS

- If you have leftovers, add this cold wild rice pilaf to pancake batter for excellent wild rice pancakes.
- If you do not have pine nuts, unsalted sunflower seeds are an excellent substitution.

RICE

Wild Rice and Pine Nut Pilaf

¼ c. butter
¼ c. shallots, diced into ¼-inch pieces
1½ c. wild rice
½ c. pine nuts
2 c. chicken stock (see recipe p. 47)
1½ tsp. Worcestershire sauce
1 c. fresh mushrooms, cut into ½-inch cubes
2 bay leaves

Preheat oven to 350°.

In a Dutch oven, heat butter. Add shallots and sauté until tender. Add wild rice and stir with a wooden spoon for 1 minute to coat rice. Add pine nuts, chicken stock, Worcestershire sauce, mushrooms and bay leaves. Stir to combine then cover. Bake in 350° oven for 1½ hours. When rice is tender, remove bay leaves and serve.

Serves 4.

- *Wild or forest mushrooms give a better flavor than button mushrooms.*

- *Remember, wild rice is a seed and does not absorb the liquid like white rice. It will not become flaky or sticky.*

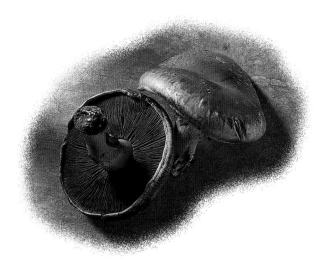

Mushroom Risotto

2 c. crimini mushrooms, sliced $\frac{1}{4}$ inch thick
$\frac{1}{4}$ c. butter
$\frac{1}{2}$ c. shallots, diced into $\frac{1}{4}$-inch pieces
2 c. uncooked medium-grained white rice
3 c. chicken stock (see recipe p. 47)
$\frac{1}{4}$ c. dry sherry wine
$\frac{1}{4}$ c. dry white wine
1 c. cream
$\frac{1}{2}$ c. Parmesan cheese, freshly grated
1 tsp. salt
$\frac{1}{4}$ tsp. freshly ground white pepper

Wash and remove stems from mushrooms. Cut into pieces. In a heavy braiser or Dutch oven, heat butter to a fast bubble. Add shallots and cook until clear. (Do not brown.) Stir in rice with a wooden spoon. Sauté until well coated (at least 2 minutes).

Combine chicken stock and wines. Add 2 cups chicken stock mixture slowly to rice. Turn heat to medium. Stir slowly until stock is absorbed and rice is almost dry. Add cream and repeat procedure. Add mushrooms and 1½ cups of stock mixture. Stir to combine and cook until rice is tender but still firm. It will appear creamy. Add Parmesan cheese, salt and pepper and fold in gently. Remove from heat. Cover and hold until service.

Serves 4 to 6.

CHEF'S TIPS
• Mushroom risotto served cold over lettuce greens and cold fish makes an excellent salad.

Rice Pilaf and Variations

1½ T. butter
2 T. red onion, diced into ¼-inch-thick pieces
1 c. long-grained white rice
2 c. chicken or fish stock (see recipe p. 47)
¼ tsp. salt
⅛ tsp. black pepper
2 bay leaves

Preheat oven to 350°.

In a Dutch oven, heat butter to a bubble. Add onion and sauté until tender. Add rice and stir with a wooden spoon for 30 seconds to coat well. Add stock, salt, pepper and bay leaves. Bring to a boil. Remove from heat. Cover with foil. Punch 8 to 10 pencil-sized holes in foil. Bake at 350° for 45 minutes. When pilaf is done, bay leaves will be on top, the liquid evaporated and the rice tender.

Serves 4.

Variations:

When adding stock:

Add ¼ c. diced ham and ½ c. green peas (frozen or fresh)
Add ¼ c. diced red pepper and ¼ c. pine nuts
Add 1 c. small, peeled raw shrimp
Add ½ c. pine nuts and 1 c. sliced fresh mushrooms

Risotto Parmesan

$^1/_4$ c. butter
$^1/_2$ c. shallots or red onions, diced into $^1/_4$-inch pieces
2 c. short-grain white rice (Arborio rice)
3$^1/_2$ c. chicken stock or fish stock (see recipe p. 47)
1 c. cream
$^1/_2$ tsp. salt
$^1/_4$ tsp. white pepper
1 tsp. poultry seasoning
$^1/_2$ c. Parmesan cheese, freshly shredded

Melt butter in a straight-sided skillet or Dutch oven. Add shallots and cook until tender. Do not brown. Add rice and stir with a wooden spoon to coat rice, about 1 minute. Slowly add 2 cups stock.

Cook over medium heat, stirring slowly until stock is absorbed. Add 1½ cups stock and repeat. Add cream, salt, white pepper and poultry seasoning. Repeating process. Remember to keep stirring slowly. Add Parmesan cheese and stir until smooth. Rice should be tender but firm. Remove from heat. Serve, or cover and keep warm.

Serves 4 to 6.

CHEF'S TIPS

- This is a recipe you can count on.
- Risotto will continue to thicken as it sits. Add stock or cream to thin the consistency.
- I love to add $^1/_2$ cup pine nuts to the risotto at the same time as the Parmesan cheese.
- There are many great variations of risotto.

CHEF'S TIPS

- If canned bean sprouts are substituted, be sure to drain them well before adding.
- Sometimes I add 2 tomatoes cut into 8 wedges with the scrambled eggs.
- Sliced red peppers are also a nice addition.

Fried Rice

2 T. peanut oil
1/2 c. red onion, cut into 1/4-inch pieces
1/2 c. celery, sliced on the bias
1/2 c. red or green peppers, cut into 1/8-inch strips
1/2 c. carrots, sliced Chinese style
1 c. fresh or frozen peas
4 c. cooked long-grain white rice
1 c. fresh bean sprouts
1 1/2 T. soy sauce
4 eggs, beaten
1/2 c. green onion, cut into 1/4-inch slices

Heat a large skillet or electric frying pan with oil to smoke-hot. Add vegetables and sauté until onion and celery start to turn clear. Do not overcook. Add rice and toss. Add bean sprouts and half the soy sauce. Toss. Add remaining soy sauce to beaten eggs. With a spatula, push rice mix to one side of the pan. Add eggs slowly to the other side of the pan. Add green onions. Scramble eggs to soft. Stir in rice and serve.

Serves 4 to 6.

Long-Grain White Rice

2 c. uncooked long-grain white rice
4 c. cold water
1 tsp. salt

Preheat oven to 350°.

Place rice in a deep bowl. Let cold water rise slowly over rice to fill bowl. Stir rice with a long-handled spoon. All rice hulls and bad kernels will float to the top. Remove floaters. Pour water and rice into a strainer.

Place rice in a medium-sized cake pan. Combine salt with cold water and pour over rice. Cover rice pan with foil and poke a dozen small holes into foil with a pencil. Place in a 350° oven for 1 hour. Water will be evaporated and rice will be tender and sticky when cooked. Remove foil. Fluff with a fork. For sticky rice, leave foil cover on after removing from oven.

Serves 4 to 6.

CHEF'S TIPS

- Short and medium-grain white rice are cooked the same way.

Chilled Rice Cakes

2 c. short-grain white rice
1/2 c. cold water
1/2 tsp. salt
1/3 c. piña colada mix
Wasabe to taste

Preheat oven to 350°.

In a medium baking dish, place rice, water and salt. Cover with aluminum foil. Punch 8 pin-sized holes in the foil. Bake in a 350° oven for 30 minutes. Remove foil and fluff rice with a fork. Add piña colada mix. Re-cover and bake for 20 more minutes.

Grease a shallow baking pan with butter. Place cooked rice in the pan and lightly press to about 1 inch thick. Top with a sheet of plastic wrap and refrigerate until chilled.

Cut into desired shape and top with cold fish fillets. Serve with a small dollop of Wasabe.

Serves 4 to 6.

CHEF'S TIPS

- This is one of the most versatile hors d'oeuvres bases.
- Wasabe is green Japanese horseradish.

DOUGHS AND CRUSTS

CHEF'S TIPS

- After you start to knead dough, the more flour you add the tougher the crust gets.
- For a great flavor, roll out the dough 1/2 inch thick. Spray with olive oil and cook on the grill.

Pizza Crust

2 c. warm water (105°)
2 T. dry yeast or two packages yeast
1 tsp. sugar

2 tsp. salt
2 T. oil
5 to 6 c. flour

This recipe makes 1 large or 2 small crusts.

In a large bowl, place warm water, dry yeast and sugar; combine. Let stand 2 minutes. Add salt, oil and half of the flour. With a large wooden spoon, mix 20 times. Gradually add flour, 1/2 cup at a time, until dough forms a mass and pulls away from the sides of the bowl. Remove dough to a floured baking cloth. Add 1/4 cup flour. If needed, add more flour a little at a time. Knead dough 50 times. Place in greased bowl. Cover with clean cloth. Set in a warm (not hot) place for one hour. Remove to greased pizza pan. Gently press into desired shape.

Top with favorite pizza fixings and bake at 400° until crust is golden brown and crisp.

CHEF'S TIPS

- Use this crust for pot pies or tops of stews.
- For pot pies, cut the dough to the size of the bowl.
- It is important to refrigerate the dough for 2 hours to allow the elasticity to relax.

Butter Pastry Dough

1/2 c. cake flour
1 1/2 c. all-purpose flour
3/4 c. butter

1/4 c. vegetable shortening
1 tsp. onion salt
1/2 c. ice water

In a large bowl, combine cake flour, all-purpose flour, butter, shortening and onion salt. Toss into pieces the size of popcorn. Add ice water and combine to make a stiff dough. Remove from bowl and knead 30 times on a lightly floured cloth. Place in plastic bag and refrigerate for 2 hours to rest. Roll out the size dough you need. For a 9-inch pie crust, about 8 ounces are needed for the bottom and 7 ounces for the top. For topping, only use 8 ounces.

Pie Crust

2 c. all-purpose flour
1 tsp. salt
1 1/4 c. shortening
2/3 c. ice water

Preheat oven to 350°.

In a large bowl, place flour and salt. Add shortening. Toss to make pieces the size of marbles. Add ice water. Lightly toss enough to make a dough. Combine dough just enough to hold together. Use a dusted pastry cloth or board for rolling out the crust.

For pie shells, dot crust with a fork. Gently shake to shrink dough. Place in pie pan. Place second pie pan on top rack. Trim excess dough from edges. Place pans in oven upside down and bake at 350° for 15 to 18 minutes. This keeps pies from blistering and bubbling.

- To make double-crust pies, bottom pie crust should weigh 8 ounces. Top crust should weigh 7 ounces for a 9-inch pie pan. Always shake crust before putting in the pie pan to prevent crust from shrinking during baking. Cut leftover dough into 8-oz. pieces and freeze in individual bags. Thaw out in refrigerator.

CHEF'S TIPS

- This recipe makes four single-crust or two double-crust 9-inch pies.
- Measure the flour accurately. Adding too much flour will make the crust tough.

CHEF'S TIPS

• I was given this recipe by a master phyllo dough maker, my friend Chef Tarek Ibrahim.

• Use premade dough whenever possible.

• It is important to use bread or high-gluten flour. Gluten is a wheat protein that gives the dough its elastic quality.

Phyllo Dough

1 c. cold water
½ tsp. salt
3 T. vegetable oil
3 c. bread flour or high-gluten flour
2 c. cornstarch for dusting

To make with a dough hook on a kitchen mixer, place water and salt together in a mixing bowl. Add oil and flour and mix 10 minutes on low speed until dough is shiny and elastic. Very lightly oil a bowl. Shape dough into a round loaf. Place in a bowl. Cover with a dish and let rest for 1 hour.

Remove dish. Put about 2 teaspoons cornstarch on a clean pastry cloth or cotton dish towel. Turn bowl upside down to release dough. Cut dough into 8 even slices like a pie. Place a generous amount of cornstarch in a small pile. Place a piece of dough, one at a time, in the cornstarch and shape into a small flat disk using the palm of your hand. Place a generous amount of cornstarch in the center of a pastry cloth. Roll each disk, one at a time, into a 10-inch-diameter circle. Stack pieces on top of each other with a generous amount of cornstarch in between. Cover with a cotton towel. When all pieces are rolled, let rest for 1 hour.

Remove cloth. With the palm of your hand press around the edge of stacked pieces using a firm, even pressure. Turn the disk over. Now from the center out, press with your flat, open hand to make a smooth disk. Using a rolling pin with an even light to medium pressure, make an X-pattern. Roll dough as thin as possible. After each X motion, gently shake the edges to relax the dough.

If dough starts to stick to cloth or rolling pin, add a little more cornstarch. Remember, this is not a contest. Go slowly. Stop rolling before the dough starts to tear. Gently lift dough and place a rod gently under dough in the center. Lift and set rod on top of two tall cereal boxes. To slightly dry, place on a cornstarch-dusted baker's cloth and place sheets on top of each other with cornstarch in between. Cover and hold for use. The layers are now ready. Use as soon as possible.

To make phyllo dough by hand

Place flour in a mound in a large mixing bowl. Make a cup-sized indention in the center. Combine salt with cold water. Place vegetable oil in indention. Add water and scoop flour over the top. Press flour down and scoop more over the top. Gently and slowly form into a wet, round loaf. Take loaf and place on a pastry sheet with ¼ cup flour and ¼ cup cornstarch and knead 100 times, rotating the loaf after each knead. Continue process as per recipe.

Chef Tarek's Tips for using commercially-made phyllo:

- Phyllo should not be frozen more than 6 months

- Thaw in refrigerator for 2 days to keep dough from cracking or tearing during unfolding

- Once sheets are removed from package, keep them covered with a damp cloth

STUFFINGS

CHEF'S TIPS

- If you do not have pastry or doughnuts to use, buy fresh pastries and doughnuts. Do not buy pre-made bread cubes. They are dry and tasteless.

- You can also use French or hard-crusted bread.

- If fresh cilantro is not available, leave it out of the recipe.

Fish and Seafood Stuffing

10 c. cubed sweet rolls, doughnuts, pastries or sourdough bread
1/2 c. butter
1 c. celery, cut into 1/4-inch slices
2 cloves garlic, minced fine
1 c. green onion cut into 1/4-inch slices
1 green Granny Smith apple, skin on, seeds removed and cut into 1/2-inch cubes
1 c. eggs
1/2 c. milk
2 tsp. Worcestershire sauce
2 tsp. chicken base
1 c. fish, chicken (see recipe p. 47) or clam broth
2 tsp. poultry seasoning
2 tsp. fresh thyme, or 1 tsp. dry thyme
1 tsp. dry sage
1 T. fresh cilantro
1/2 tsp. black pepper
1 tsp. lemon zest, grated

Preheat oven to 350°.

Cut pastries or bread into 1-inch cubes. Heat a skillet with butter. Add celery and garlic and sauté for 1 minute. Add green onions and sauté until clear and tender. Add apples and combine. Remove from skillet and place in a large bowl. Add 8 cups pastry cubes. In a blender cup, place eggs, milk, Worcestershire sauce, chicken base, broth, seasonings and lemon zest. Combine on low for 20 seconds.

Add mixture to bread/vegetable mixture. Combine with a large spoon. Add remaining 2 cups pastry cubes and combine. If stuffing seems too loose, add a few pastry cubes at a time to the mixture. If stuffing is too dry, add a little milk. Place in refrigerator for 20 minutes to absorb liquid. Adjust consistency and either stuff fish or bake stuffing in a covered container for 1 1/2 hours at 350°.

Makes 2 quarts.

Cornbread Stuffing

1/2 c. salted butter
1 1/2 c. red onion, cut into 1/4-inch pieces
2 cloves garlic, minced fine
1 c. celery, cut into 1/4-inch slices
1 c. yellow or red peppers, cut into 1/4-inch cubes
1/2 c. sweet gherkin pickles, cut into 1/4-inch cubes
1/4 c. sunflower seeds
6 c. cubed corn bread, cut into 1/2-inch cubes
3 eggs, beaten
1 c. chicken or fish stock (see recipe p. 47)
2 tsp. dry thyme
1 tsp. dry tarragon
1 tsp. dry poultry seasoning
2 tsp. Worcestershire sauce
1/2 tsp. salt
1/2 tsp. black pepper
1 c. fresh pears, peeled, cut into 1/2-inch cubes

Preheat oven to 350°.

In a large skillet, heat butter to a fast bubble. Add onions, garlic, celery and peppers. Sauté until onions are tender. Add pickles and sunflower seeds. Turn heat to low and simmer 10 minutes. Place in a large mixing bowl. Add cornbread and toss to combine. Do not overmix.

In a large bowl, place eggs, stock, seasonings, Worcestershire sauce, salt and pepper. Whisk to combine well. Add pears and cornbread mixture. Combine well. Place in a Dutch oven or covered baking dish. Bake stuffing in a 350° oven for about 1 hour.

Makes 1 1/2 quarts.

Variations

To Make Maryland Style:
Add 2 c. raw oysters and liquid as the last step. Very gently fold in the stuffing

For Southwestern Style:
Add seeded hot chili peppers, cut into 1/4-inch cubes

For Heartland Style:
Add 1 c. pork sausage with vegetables in first step

For Canadian Style:
Add 1 1/2 c. smoked salmon pieces as the last step

CHEF'S TIPS

• For stuffing a whole fish, cool the stuffing in the refrigerator first, stuff the fish and bake. Excess stuffing can be frozen in double-thick sealable plastic bags.

CHEF'S TIPS

• I love my dumplings with a ton of butter!

Baking Powder Dumplings

2 large eggs, beaten
¼ c. milk
½ tsp. salt
2 T. melted butter
1 c. flour
1 T. cream of wheat or farina
2 tsp. baking powder

Beat eggs to a froth. Add milk, salt and butter. Combine flour, cream of wheat and baking powder. Add to liquid. Gently mix to combine. Do not overmix.

Dip large spoon into boiling liquid (water, broth, soup, etc.). Dip spoon into batter and drop into boiling liquid. Continue until batter is gone. Cover and simmer 12 to 15 minutes.

Serves 4.

Variations:

Add 2 tsp. fresh dill
Add 2 tsp. fresh herbs
Add 2 tsp. Parmesan cheese
Add 2 tsp. diced shallots (cooked and cooled)
Add 3 tsp. shredded cheese

CHEF'S TIPS

• A nice touch is to remove the crusts from the baked cheese slices before cutting into the triangles. The crust pieces make an excellent snack for the chef.

Cheese Croutons

8 slices English muffin or sourdough bread
2 T. soft butter
1 c. shredded cheese

Preheat oven to 375°.

Butter English muffin or sourdough bread slice with butter on both sides. Place on a baking sheet. Shred your favorite cheese over the top of each slice as thick or thin as you wish. Bake in a 375° oven until cheese is melted or light brown. Remove from pan and cut into triangles.

Serves 4.

• *For a spicier version, add a few hot pepper slices on top of the cheese.*

Grandma Blenda and Betty Crocker's Square Biscuits

2 c. flour
1 T. baking powder
1 tsp. salt
1/4 c. vegetable shortening

2 T. butter
2/3 c. milk
1/2 tsp. pure vanilla extract

Preheat oven to 450°.

Combine flour, baking powder and salt. In a large mixing bowl, add shortening and butter and toss until it has a texture of meal. Add vanilla to milk. Sprinkle evenly over base. Rub your hand with a little butter or shortening and combine mixture into a soft, puffy dough. Place dough on a lightly floured baker's cloth. Knead gently exactly 6 times. Pat dough to 1/2-inch thickness. Cut into 2-inch squares. Place on a lightly greased baking pan at 450° for 10 to 12 minutes.

Serve immediately or place in a bowl with a cotton dish towel covering the top. The cotton cloth will let the steam escape.

Serves 4 to 6.

CHEF'S TIPS

• My grandmother cut biscuits into squares so there were no dough pieces to reshape and recut.

MISCELLANEOUS

CHEF'S TIPS

• This recipe is an easy one to take with on a trip. Put the dry ingredients in a sealable plastic bag and the wet ingredients in a double sealable plastic bag. Pour dry ingredients into wet bag, shake and put into hot skillet. You can add your favorite fixings such as chili peppers, sunflower seeds or sun-dried tomatoes.

Rich, Cheesy Cornbread

2 eggs
2 egg yolks
¼ c. butter, melted
2 c. milk
1 c. sour cream
2 c. cream-style corn
1 T. sugar
1 tsp. onion salt
¼ tsp. white pepper
1 tsp. orange zest, grated
1 c. longhorn-style colby cheese, grated
1 c. flour
1¼ c. cornmeal, yellow or white
1 tsp. poultry seasoning
1 tsp. baking powder
½ tsp. baking soda

Preheat oven to 350°. Put a medium-sized cast-iron skillet in the oven for at least 15 minutes.

In a bowl, place eggs, yolks, melted butter, milk, sour cream, corn, sugar, salt, pepper, orange zest and grated cheese. With a wooden spoon, stir to combine well. Combine flour, cornmeal, poultry seasoning, baking powder and baking soda. Add to wet mixture and stir well to combine.

Brush or spray hot skillet with olive oil. Add batter to about ¾ full. Bake for 25 minutes. Remove from oven. Set on a cooling rack and brush top with a light butter coat. Place a clean cotton towel on top. Latent heat will finish cooking the bread. Let cool for 10 minutes. Cut in slabs and serve with butter and honey.

Serves 4.

Pearl Barley Pilaf with Sun-Dried Tomatoes

1/2 c. butter
1 c. onion, diced into 1/4-inch pieces
2 cloves garlic, diced into 1/4-inch pieces
1 c. uncooked pearl barley
1/2 c. sun-dried tomato pieces

3 c. chicken stock (see recipe p. 47) or clam broth
2 bay leaves
1/2 tsp. salt
1/4 tsp. black pepper
1 tsp. fresh thyme
1 T. Worcestershire sauce

Preheat oven to 350°.

In a Dutch oven, melt butter. Add onions and garlic and cook until tender. Add barley. Stir with a wooden spoon to coat with butter for 1½ to 2 minutes. Add sun-dried tomatoes, 3 cups stock, 2 bay leaves, salt, pepper, thyme and Worcestershire sauce. Stir well to combine. Cover pot with a sheet of aluminum foil. Punch 8 pinhole-sized holes in foil. Place in 350° oven for 1½ hours. Remove from oven. Remove bay leaves. Toss with a fork. Hold for service.

Serves 4 to 6.

Polenta

3 c. water
1/2 tsp. salt

2 T. butter
1 c. yellow cornmeal

Preheat oven to 350°.

Bring water, salt and butter to a boil in a heavy saucepot or Dutch oven. Sprinkle in cornmeal while stirring constantly. Add cornmeal slowly so it will not lump. When thick, cover and bake in a 350° oven for 20 to 25 minutes. If you are at a campsite, keep stirring until your arm almost falls off or about 20 minutes, whichever comes first.

Spoon into bowls and top with butter and brown sugar. If polenta is to be fried, pour batter into a buttered baking pan and spread smooth. Cool and cut into desired shape. Pan-fry or grill to eat.

Serves 4.

CHEF'S TIPS

• All fresh vegetables, cut into 1/4-inch cubes, are excellent in this recipe.

CHEF'S TIPS

• For gourmet polenta, add 1/2 cup diced shallots and 1/2 cup grated Parmesan cheese before putting polenta in the oven.

CHEF'S TIPS

• I got this recipe
  in the submarine
  service from my
  leading commissary
  man, Soupy
  Campbell.

• These beans are
  great hot or cold.

Soupy Campbell Beans

15-oz. can kidney beans
15.5-oz. can butter beans
2 15-oz. cans pork and beans
1 c. brown sugar
1¼ c. onion, cut into small pieces
½ c. ketchup
2 tsp. yellow mustard
⅓ c. dill pickle juice
¼ c. maple syrup

Place all ingredients into a heavy pot. Simmer, uncovered, on low heat for 30 minutes, or until onions are tender, stirring gently to prevent beans from sticking to the bottom of the pot.

Serves 4.

CHEF'S TIPS

• Johnny cakes and
  hush puppies use
  the same recipe.
  Johnny cakes are
  cooked on a griddle.
  Hush puppies are
  fried in oil.

• To make hush
  puppies that bite,
  add diced chili
  peppers that bark.

Johnny Cakes and Hush Puppies

1 egg	1 tsp. baking powder
2 egg yolks	¼ tsp. ground nutmeg
1 tsp. salt	1 tsp. pure vanilla extract
2 c. cornmeal	1¼ c. milk

Heat an electric griddle to 375°.

In a bowl, beat eggs and yolks. Add salt and half the cornmeal. Stir to combine. Add baking powder and nutmeg to rest of the cornmeal. Add cornmeal mixture and vanilla to base. Add milk and stir until smooth. If batter is too thick, add milk one tablespoon at a time to thin. Drop a tablespoon of batter on a 375° griddle. Fry until brown on both sides and serve with hot butter, brown sugar or jam.

To make hush puppies, use the same recipe but add 1 cup diced onions and a little more cornmeal. Form into small cakes the size of a biscuit. Use a ¼-cup measure scoop to form puppies. Fry puppies in 1 inch of oil at 375°. Drain on a paper towel and serve hot.

Serves 4.

Spätzle

4 eggs
¼ c. cold water
½ tsp. salt
¼ tsp. ground nutmeg
1¾ c. flour
2 qts. water for boiling with
2 tsp. salt

Break four eggs in a medium-sized bowl. Add water, salt and nutmeg. Beat with a wire whisk until frothy. Add flour slowly until the mixture is stiff and gathers around the whisk. Remove any mixture from whisk and continue stirring with a spoon until mixture comes off the sides of the bowl.

Bring salted water to a boil. Put dough into a spätzle maker and drop into water. Return water to a boil and simmer for 1 minute. Remove spätzle from boiling water and rinse under cold water. Drain well. Line pan with a dry cotton towel. Place spätzle on towel and cover until ready to use.

To serve, melt butter in a skillet and sauté spätzle until hot, being careful not to brown. Spätzle may also be served with pan gravy.

Serves 4 to 6.

- *This dish is one of the supreme contributions of German cuisine to world cooking. It is not hard to make but it should be approached with respect and care.*

- *You can make a number of variations to this classic side dish by adding chopped parsley, bacon bits, salt, nutmeg, minced onions, shallots and Parmesan cheese while sautéing.*

CHEF'S TIPS

- If you don't have a spätzle maker, make a homemade version by pressing dough through a deep fryer basket.
- Spätzle keeps for about four days in refrigerator.

CHEF'S TIPS

• To make grilled grits cakes, place warm cooked grits in a buttered shallow baking pan. Refrigerate until cold. Cut into squares or cookie cutter shapes. To serve, sauté in butter until golden brown on both sides.

Grits Supreme

¹⁄₄ c. butter
¹⁄₂ c. shallots, diced into ¹⁄₄-inch pieces
1 c. chicken stock (see recipe p. 38)
2 c. heavy cream
¹⁄₂ tsp. salt
¹⁄₄ tsp. white pepper
1 tsp. poultry seasoning
1 c. uncooked grits
¹⁄₂ c. Parmesan cheese, grated

In a heavy saucepan, heat butter to a fast bubble. Add shallots and cook until tender. Add chicken stock, cream, salt, pepper and poultry seasoning. Slowly add grits. Stir with a wooden spoon. Cook on low heat for 5 minutes. Add Parmesan cheese and cook 5 minutes. Cover to keep hot until serving.

Serves 4 to 6.

NOTES

CULINARY TERMS

SOURCES: *Webster's New World Dictionary of Culinary Arts by Labensky, Ingram and Labensky and Food Lover's Companion by Sharon Tyler Herbst*

Balsamic Vinegar - A dark, mellow Italian vinegar with a sweet-sour flavor; made from concentrated grape juice, fermented and aged for 15 to 20 years in a series of wooden casks.

Beurre Noir - French for black butter. Used to describe butter cooked until dark brown (not black); sometimes flavored with vinegar or lemon juice, capers and parsley, and served over fish, eggs and vegetables.

Beurre Noisette - French for brown butter. Used to describe butter cooked until it is light hazelnut (noisette) color; flavored and used in much the same manner as beurre noir.

Blini - Pancakes, usually of buckwheat or rye flour.

Broth - A flavorful liquid obtained from the long simmering of meats and/or vegetables.

Capers - The unopened flower buds of a shrub native to the Mediterranean region; after curing in salted white vinegar, the buds develop a sharp, salty-sour flavor and are used as a flavoring and condiment.

Chutney - A condiment made from fruit, vinegar, sugar and spices; its texture can range from smooth to chunky and its flavor from mild to hot.

Compote - Fresh or dried fruit cooked in a sugar syrup.

Confiture - French for jam, jelly, marmalade or fruit preserves.

Coulis - A sauce made from a puree of vegetables or fruit; may be hot or cold.

Court Bouillon - Water simmered with vegetables, seasonings and an acidic liquid such as vinegar or wine; used for simmering or poaching fish, shellfish or vegetables.

Crimini Mushrooms - Italian for various common store mushrooms.

Demi-Glace - French for half-glaze. Used to describe a mixture of half brown stock and half brown sauce reduced by half.

Dice - To cut food into cubes (large dice = 5/8-in. cubes, medium dice = 3/8-in. cubes, small dice = 1/4-in. cubes.)

Dredging - Coating a food with flour or finely ground crumbs; usually done prior to sautéing or frying or as the first step of the standarized breading procedure.

Dutch Oven - A large kettle, typically made of cast iron, with a tight-fitting lid; used for stewing or braising.

Egg Wash - A mixture of beaten eggs (whole eggs, yolk or whites) and a liquid, usually milk or water. Used to coat doughs before baking to add sheen.

Fish Sauce - A thin, dark-brown liquid made from anchovy extract and salt; used as a flavoring, it has a very salty flavor and a strong, pungent aroma.

Ghee - A form of clarified butter originating in India.

Grinder - Any of a variety of manual or electrical devices used to reduce food to small particles of varying degrees by the action of rotating blades; also known as a mill. In some regions, "grinder" also refers to a huge sandwich.

Heavy Saucepan - Has one long handle, straight to slightly bowled sides. Used for range-top cooking.

Herbed Salad Dressing - An herbed sauce for a salad. Most are cold and are based on a vinaigrette, mayonnaise or other emulsified product.

Julienne - To cut a food into a matchstick shape of approximately 1/8 in. x 1/8 in. x 1/2 in.

Leek - Member of the lily family; has a thick, cylindrical white stalk with a slightly bulbous root end and many flat, dull dark green leaves. The tender white stalk has a flavor that is sweeter and stronger than a green onion but milder than an onion and is used in salads and as a flavoring.

Mince - To cut or chop a food finely.

Napa Cabbage - A member of the cabbage family with a stout, elongated head of relatively tightly packed, firm, crinkly, pale yellow-green leaves with a thick white center vein and mild, delicate flavor; also known as chard cabbage, Chinese cabbage and snow cabbage.

Okra - The seed pod of a tropical plant of the hollyhock family native to Africa. The oblong, tapering pod has ridged green skin, a flavor reminiscent of asparagus and is used like a vegetable in African and southern U.S. cuisines. Because it develops a gelatinous texture if cooked for long periods, it is also used as a thickener.

On The Bias - Cut on a line diagonal to the grain.

Paella - A rustic Spanish dish of rice, vegetables, sausages, poultry, fish and shellfish seasoned with saffron.

Parsley Sprig - A small shoot; twig.

Pesto - An Italian pasta sauce made from basil, garlic, olive oil, pine nuts and Parmesan.

Plum Tomato - An egg-shaped tomato with a meaty flesh and a red skin (a yellow variety is also available); also known as an Italian tomato or Roma tomato.

Poaching - A moist-heat cooking method that uses convection to transfer heat from a hot liquid to the food submerged in it.

Puff Pastry - A rich, flaky pastry made by enclosing fat, usually butter, in a sheet of dough, rolling the dough out, and continuing to fold and roll the dough until many thin layers of fat and dough are created. As it bakes, the layers rise and separate slightly, due to the steam released by the fat.

Puree - To process food to achieve a smooth pulp; food that is processed by mashing, straining or fine chopping to achieve a smooth pulp.

Roe - A collective term for the spawn of female fish (also known as the hard roe), the milt of male fish (also known as soft roe) or the eggs contained within the fish's or shellfish's ovarian membrane.

Roux - A cooked mixture of equal parts flour and fat, by weight, used as thickener for sauces, soups and other dishes. Cooking the flour in fat coats the starch granules with the fat and prevents them from forming lumps when introduced into a liquid.

Saffron Aïoli - A garlic mayonnaise made in France's Provence region with a spice that is the dried yellow-orange stigma of a crocus's purple flower.

Salt Pork - Very fatty pork, usually from the hog's sides and belly, cured in salt and used principally as a cooking fat or flavoring; also known as corned belly bacon and white bacon.

Sambals - Any of several very spicy mixtures or relishes based on chilis; used in Indian and Southeast Asian cuisines as a flavoring and condiment.

Sauté Pan - A fry pan with sloping sides. Long handle for easier flipping.

Sautéing - A dry-heat cooking method that uses conduction to transfer heat from a hot pan to food with the aid of a small amount of hot fat; cooking is usually done quickly over high temperatures.

Sear - To brown a food quickly over high heat; usually done as a preparatory step for combination cooking methods.

Shallot - A member of the onion family native to the Middle East and formed like garlic with a head composed of several cloves covered in a thin papery skin. The outer covering can be pale brown, bronze, pale gray or rose with a pink-tinged, ivory-colored flesh and a flavor that is more subtle than an onion and less harsh than garlic.

Simmering - Maintaining the temperature of a liquid just below the boiling point.

Skillet - Heavy, thick-bottomed frying pan, usually cast iron, or a cast-iron skillet, also called Griswold.

Smoke Point - The temperature at which a fat begins to break down, releasing an acrid blue gas and giving a burned flavor to food.

Stock - A clear, unthickened liquid flavored by soluble substances extracted from meat, poultry or fish and their bones as well as from a mirepoix, other vegetables and seasonings; used for soups and sauces.

Tempura - A Japanese dish of battered and deep-fried pieces of fish and vegetables, usually accompanied by a sauce.

Three-Pepper-Blend - white, green and black peppercorns.

Velouté - A French leading sauce made by thickening a veal stock, chicken stock of fish fumet with a white or golden roux; also known as blond sauce.

Wasabe - A green Japanese horseradish-like root.

Zest - Strips of rind from a citrus fruit; the colored, outermost layer of citrus rind used for flavoring cream, custards and baked goods.

INDEX

Good for the Stomach and the Spirit

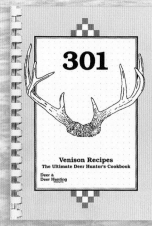

301 Venison Recipes
The Ultimate Deer Hunter's Cookbook
by Deer & Deer Hunting Staff
Mouth-watering recipes have made this cookbook a hunter's classic. Look no further for delicious meals that will feed a hungry bunch at deer camp, or serve special guests at home.
Comb-bound • 6 x 9 • 128 pages
Item# VR01 • $10.95

Dinner a Day: Slow Cooker
365 Appetizing and Affordable Meals Your Family Will Love
by Margaret Kaeter
Whether you're at the cabin in the summer or during hunting season, or just looking for something good to eat that's ready when you are, the delicious dishes in this book will make your mouth water. Check out Cuban Black Bean Stew, Beef Bourguignon and Pepperoni Rigatoni, among others.
Comb-bound • 6 x 8-1/2 • 416 pages
Item# Z1748 • $16.95

The Everything®
Wild Game Cookbook
From fowl and fish to rabbit and venison
by Karen Eagle
Get the low down on cooking exotic catches including deer, wild boar, buffalo, pheasant, and freshwater fish, among others. Review tips and hints for preparing meat (roasting and smoking) using rubs and relishes, and learn about complimentary sides and desserts.
Softcover • 8 x 9-1/4 x 304 pages
Item# 545-X • $14.95

Classic Deer Camps
by Robert Wegner
Revisit 19th century deer camps through the spectacular collection of writings, historical biographies of famous deer camp and stellar nostalgic artwork in this beautiful book.
Hardcover • 8-1/4 x 10-7/8 • 224 pages
50 b&w photos • 100 color photos
Item# Z2051 • $29.99

Warman's®
Sporting Collectibles
Identification and Price Guide
by Russell E. Lewis
Take a trip back in time with this beautifully illustrated guide of vintage sporting goods and gear, including everything from shot shell boxes and fishing lures, to pheasant stamps and archery posters.
Softcover • 8-1/4 x 10-7/8 • 256 pages
1,200 color photos
Item# Z1022 • $24.99

Order directly from the publisher at www.krausebooks.com

Krause Publications, Offer OTB9
P.O. Box 5009
Iola, WI 54945-5009
www.krausebooks.com

Call 800-258-0929 M-F 8 a.m. - 5 p.m. to order direct from the publisher, or shop booksellers nationwide and select outdoors shops.
Please reference offer OTB9 with all direct-to-publisher orders

Hunting How-To and News at www.deeranddeerhunting.com